Praise for
Subversive Catholicism

"Martin Mosebach is a writer with profound Catholic sensibilities. These reflections on the 21st-century Church are expertly cut gems. A must read."—R. R. RENO, Editor, *First Things*

"Martin Mosebach employs his brilliance to defend what is of eternal value. His deep appreciation of the Catholic faith is manifest in these essays that draw upon his love of history, art, philosophy, and popular religious culture. He has a salutary horror of innovation and novelty in the life of the Church: 'When a Catholic hears the concept "new" used in relation to the Church, he should always be alarmed. The sole new and novel event of world history—the incarnation of God—has already occurred.' Christ's presence is mystically experienced in the timeless sacred liturgy of the Church. Misguided reforms have deprived the Church of that serenity of belief and life. Mosebach guides us on the way to recover our love and reverence for what was cast aside in the frenzied search for relevance after the Second Vatican Council. Bravo!"—FR. GERALD MURRAY, Pastor, Church of the Holy Family, NYC

"In this collection of essays, Martin Mosebach has once more demonstrated his ability to provide provocative insights into the condition of modern Catholicism. He notes the tension—found in both East and West—between the liturgical principle that the rites be 'fear-inspiring' and the modern worshipper who 'relaxes in an armchair waiting for [God] to arrive.' He suggests that the needs of the ordinary believer are satisfied, if at all, in the kitsch products of Lourdes gift-shops, while elite Catholicism offers him an empty aesthetic puritanism. He suggests that the supplanting of the monarch by the people as wielder of sovereignty makes for fiscal profligacy. He explores the parallel between prayer wheels of oriental religions and church bells of European Christianity. These essays are a tonic to our deep-rutted discourse on liturgy, spirituality, and religious sociology. Refreshing and challenging, they set us on new paths of thought."—JOSEPH SHAW, Chairman, Latin Mass Society of England & Wales

"*Subversive Catholicism* is the first complete English-language translation of a collection, first published in 2012, of Martin Mosebach's essays on a broad range of topics, all involving the Church. It offers a treasure trove of insights on liturgy, theology, art, ecclesiastical government, and contemporary spiritual issues. All is short and sweet, reflecting the concise yet amazingly versatile style of a true master of prose. *Subversive Catholicism* does not repeat platitudes or reinforce received opinions—it makes you think. And given the present state of the Church, this book is more relevant today than it was in 2012!"—STUART CHESSMAN, President, Society of St. Hugh of Cluny

"Germany's most distinguished living Catholic writer is a novelist who seems almost to have wandered into our time from the 19th century. But it is precisely because his mind is so out of keeping with our time that he is able to understand it so well, as these delightful and penetrating essays show."—PATER EDMUND WALDSTEIN, O.Cist., Vice-Rector, Leopoldinum, Heiligenkreuz

Subversive Catholicism

Papacy, Liturgy, Church

Subversive CATHOLICISM

PAPACY, LITURGY, CHURCH

✦ ✦ ✦

Martin Mosebach

Translated by
Sebastian Condon &
Graham Harrison

Angelico Press

First Published in German as
Der Ultramontane – Alle Wege führen nach Rom
© Paulinus Verlag, Gmbh, Trier, 2012
First published in English by Angelico Press, 2019
Copyright © Angelico Press 2019

All rights reserved

No part of this book may be reproduced or transmitted,
in any form or by any means, without permission.

For information, address:
Angelico Press
169 Monitor St.
Brooklyn, NY 11222
info@angelicopress.com
www.angelicopress.com

978-1-62138-443-4 (pbk)
978-1-62138-444-1 (cloth)
978-1-62138-445-8 (ebook)

Cover design: Michael Schrauzer

CONTENTS

PART I: THE POPE IN ROME

Ultramontane 1

The Chinese Pope 5

Pope Without a Country 11

He Is, After All, Only the Pope 15

On the Pope 25

PART II: LITURGY IN THE CHURCH

Prayer 41

> Praying and Dying [41]—The Churchy Type and "Pius Aeneas" [43]—The Necessity of Prayer Wheels [46]—"Oculis levatis ad caelum" [47]—The Repetitions of the Angel [51]

Christmas Every Day 55

By Their Fruits You Shall Know Them… 59

> The break with tradition [59]—The new Mass is not the Mass of Vatican II [60]—The aim of the reform was not to strengthen discipline but to weaken it [62]—By its own standards the "pastoral" reform of the Mass has failed [63]—The reform of the Mass will not stand up to detailed examination [64]—The reform of the Mass has produced poisonous fruit [66]

The Old Roman Missal: Between Loss
and Rediscovery 69

Return to Form: The Fate of the Rite is
the Fate of the Church 87

PART III: CHRISTIANS IN THE WORLD

God Must Be in Europe's Constitution 103

The Anarchism of Mercy 107

On the Value of Proscription 113

A German Pilgrim in Chartres 119

A Magical Place: Lourdes and the Pilgrims 125

    The City and the Churches [125]—The Ritual [127]—Bernadette [129]—The Pilgrims [132]—The House of Bernadette's Parents [134]—Kitsch [136]—The Grotto [138]

In Praise of the Lourdes Madonna 141

PART I

The Pope in Rome

Ultramontane

The word "ultramontane" that rolls so well off tongue and lips, shares the same fate as many words of foreign origin that once seemed indispensable. At one time such catchwords were used even by people who did not understand a word of Latin; in the passage of time they became rare antiques before, ultimately, they were entirely forgotten. In the nineteenth century, when Prussia began to overstep its banks, as it were, and inundate Germany, a Prussian-style Germany came into being, violating German history and ejecting an Austria that had been part of the traditionally Catholic lands. In the south and west of this new Protestant empire there remained a Catholic residue that, while it was too small to threaten Prussian hegemony, was yet large enough to obstruct the homogeneity to which Prussia aspired. Anyone who was not happy to live within the structures of the new state was suspected of being hostile to the empire. These enemies of empire made strange bedfellows: they included reactionary Guelphs, socialists, liberals, old-Prussian conservatives and, indeed, "ultramontanes." Something of ill omen clung to the ultramontanes: the suspicion of treason. They were accused of having a divided loyalty that was only half (or less) attached to the Prussian emperor, while the other half (or more) was attached "beyond the mountains"—*ultra montes*—in Rome, to the pope. And perhaps there was something in this charge. For instance, the Catholic bishops refused to acknowledge the Prussian view that marriage was a contract between citizens—a view that was now meant to be binding on all Germans. For them, marriage was not a Prussian invention of positive law but a sacrament that had been instituted in paradise before the beginning of all history. At that time Catholic bishops went to prison for their convictions,

Subversive Catholicism

while the Prussian monarch tried to reinterpret Cologne Cathedral as a national icon of Prussian Germany.

This *Kulturkampf* ("culture struggle") that lasted for a hundred and thirty years is now unimaginably distant; today we can reconstruct it only with great difficulty. The very idea that, at that time, there could have been "ultramontane Germans" has become utterly improbable. The present German Catholic Church, at all events, is no longer ultramontane. It is most definitely *not* ultramontane. Today when, in serious political circles, it is quite impossible to speak of Prussian-German, or even of merely German nationalism, it is probably only the German Catholic Church that assumes the right to mark out a specifically German path, unafraid of finding itself in opposition to Rome.

Once its historical context has disappeared, a political concept becomes not only superfluous: it also becomes liberated from that context. If we look more closely, we shall see that what is "ultramontane" conserves features of Catholic existence that are independent of the Prussian-Catholic conflict known to history—and that are actually part of the core of the Catholic understanding and life-awareness.

The fundamental Catholic approach to life remains unchanged amid the mutations of historico-political conditions; the Catholic could resonate with Joséphine Baker's famous chanson "J'ai deux amours" ("I have two loves"). In part he is a child of the country that bore him: its language and history fashion his thinking and he is committed to its constitutional order; but in part—to whatever degree—he is a citizen of Rome, the city of the pope. His loyalty to the pope is at least equal to his loyalty to his native land.

The concept of the "ultras" comes from the time of the Bourbon restoration after Napoleon's demise: the "ultras" were the reactionary party of whom it was said that "they had learned nothing and forgotten nothing." While it is probable that the "ultramontanes" were so called after these "ultras," they have little in common. They are fundamentally alien to one another, because the ultramontane simply cannot be committed unconditionally to any political party. His loyalty to the Roman pope prohibits that kind of identification that characterizes the real "party" man. The ultramontane lives by the conviction that the society of his homeland cannot have the last word in matters of rights, justice, and morality. It has no power, of itself, to generate its own legitimacy; it cannot constitute a seamless, hermetically sealed-off system that is purely self-referential. Ultramontanism is the great antitotalitarian refusal: the ultramontane does not regard the medieval battles between emperor and pope as belonging to a historical epoch, but as a paradigm valid for the present and the future.

What distinguishes the ultramontane is that he does not cling to an idea: he does not dream of an Eternal Rome that is the realm of a Christian civilization (and against which he judges his historical present); no, he is attached to a human being, the pope, who makes concrete the Roman claim and, by doing so, withdraws it from the speculation of the educated elite. Nothing, perhaps, is more opposed to the influence of "the times" than this loyalty—not to a mere thing, concept, or idea, but to a person of flesh and blood.

Politically, as the past makes plain, this attitude does not necessarily bring peace and harmony. In countries that are divided in terms of religion, or are largely secularized, an unbridgeable dissent is created: when it comes to deciding which power is to be invoked to assert what is ultimately morally binding, there can be no compromise. All the same we should remember that the twofold authority of pope and state can also have dire consequences for lands that are homogeneous in terms of religion: who knows how much anarchy and chaos, in rootedly Catholic countries such as Colombia and Peru, is due to a practical ultramontanism? Such insights and issues do not need to upset the ultramontane: he does not set his heart on the creation of political harmony on earth; he considers tension and unrest to be germane to the situation in which we live.

The Chinese Pope

CHARLES BAUDELAIRE dubbed the great Voltaire "prédicateur des concierges"—the caretaker's preacher—in order to characterize the phenomenon of an Enlightenment that had exercised its influence at the level of the proletariat. For the twentieth century, Hegel took on the conscious role of the preacher. In the twentieth century, in the worldview of the Hegelian caretaker, there was nothing to be seen but progress. First monarchy fought against democracy, then fascism fought against communism, then capitalism fought against bolshevism and in each case there was a clear victor and the attainment of a new stage, in the sense of a progression that comprised a palpable step up from each previous stage. And it ought, actually, to continue in the same way: now the nation will fight against the global state: a great, borderless consumer paradise is fast approaching. Even the anti-communist caretakers of all classes had a blessed final state in mind which was surprisingly comparable to the millenarian fantasies of Karl Marx, maligned by them though he was. Actually, almost all competing parties shared a fundamental conviction: Voltaire's "Écrasez l'infâme!"—the manifesto of abolishing religion, or at least confining it within "socially acceptable" boundaries—was common to them all.

If the omens do not deceive, it would seem that the mentality of the Hegelian caretaker is disappearing as part of that mysterious process that belongs to the unfathomable regularity of history and which protects no mentality for more than one hundred years. The conception of progress, gnawing its way triumphantly into the future, has in the meantime engendered in many people mysterious terror rather than hope. To the extent that the economic machinery occasionally inclines to fits of

Subversive Catholicism

coughing, people discover their love for the status quo. Can't everything just remain, for a while, as it is? Engineers of progress are turned into pensioners of progress: one could wish that "progress"—at least within the small, Western edge of the Eurasian landmass that was once called the Occident—might have a few peaceful twilight years. In the meantime, some have now realized that this cannot be. What was accepted about notions of progress was the ceaseless and irresistible movement of history; only the partisans of the religion that is progress believed they knew which direction this movement would take. This certainty, as the prevailing mood of an epoch, appears to be in decline. It is perhaps symptomatic that it is felt to be ever more necessary to warn the public of "blind anti-Americanism," often by those self-same authors who in their earlier years criticized a "blind anti-Communism." At the height of American power doubts are now starting to arise as to North America being, for some while yet and with undiminished power, the engine of progress. It is as if the fascination that the culture of the United States aroused in Europe is beginning to fade. At the same time, Europe is distancing itself from the plan of political unity. The sense that great changes are afoot in the political sphere—changes which seem threatening and untamable—triggers in our contemporaries the drive to hold fast to something; like passengers on a ship swaying amidst a storm. While the waning Roman Empire could have placed hope in the barbarians and their surplus energy, those barbarians would today be invited in, in the hope of guaranteeing the further payment of annuities. At the same time, the industrially developed nations are staring with fear and incomprehension upon an Islam in whose form Religion—thought to have been completely tamed—is once again suddenly raising its head. They no longer have a religion of their own with which to oppose it; the clergy themselves have long since abandoned every pretense at making religion an issue of importance in the public square. The German "Lehmann-Church" (which has an equivalent in the majority of Western nations) combines the degeneration of

The Chinese Pope

the Church (now an open community of worldviews) with vague philanthropic engagement. It is thus neither Christian faith nor the legal order created by Rome that is perceived as endangered by Islam, but rather certain Western "values," which must of course be something other than the national culture, language, the Christian religion, and the law that is particular to Europe; indeed, the cherished "values" now seem to stand distinctly opposed to those very things. There has yet to be any evidence submitted to show that the "threat to Western values" means any more than "Islam wishes to deprive us of our porn."

Each passing year invites speculation as to the future, yet this time it would seem that there is limited enthusiasm for imagining the options available in the upcoming year. The clinging clay of the present age is stubbornly refusing to disclose what form the future may take. All elements within the political constellation are of course readily known, as if they were pieces on a chessboard with precisely constrained possibilities of movement. Does the world—now become so small—still retain caverns in which unsuspected energies are stored? Is there yet another power which could lend history a completely novel and astounding turn?

Chesterton once imagined the political calculations and plans of an exalted Byzantine bureaucrat around the year AD 570, plans that would have included the dangers presented by the Bulgars, the Goths, and the Scythians: yet in his calculations he would not have been able to make allowance for the fact that in the same year, far beyond the borders of the Byzantine Empire in the city of Mecca, a boy by the name of Mohammed would be born who was destined to change the face of the world. Realism demands a certain calculation of the incalculable, yet even without over-straining the imagination we can see that the world, in its existing and well-known personalities, has sufficient potential for enormous incursions into the trusted—if increasingly fragile—order. For example we can imagine—almost as a more aerial form of the tradi-

Subversive Catholicism

tional pouring of lead on New Year's Eve—that, after the death of the currently reigning pope (may the Lord grant him a long life!),[1] a Chinaman might emerge from the conclave as the new pope. Such an election is not out of the question: after the pope from Poland the Italian privilege has been broken and the election of an African or South American has long since been conceived—so why not a pope from China? He would be the first pope since Emperor Constantine who would once again come from a persecuted Church; a pope, who has possibly made the acquaintance of prison and detention; a priest who has literally had his integrity tested in fire; not an exponent of a functionary Church, embedded within some Roman College of Nobles; a priest who would never have sat on a talk-show or at a session of the broadcasting commission. A Chinese pope would never, prior to his election, have found himself in any cozy national consensus; never have experienced the temptations which arise out of the corrupting cooperation of the Church and the secularized state. He would be the representative of a Church which accepts death and persecution for the confession of faith; a Church which has no sympathy whatsoever for the abolition of religion by theologians and which sees its mission in prayer and not in the articulation of "invitations to dialogue" and in the "achievement of contributions to a more just society." A pope for whom his own obedience, as well as that of others, probably has a particularly heavy emphasis: a man of monk-like asceticism with a pronounced sense of the discipline of the rites. Probably a reticent, in any case not overly voluble pope. This, however, is only the aspect of such an election that might principally interest Catholics. A different choice might conceivably bring about the end of everything we are familiar with.

    Let us then proceed resolutely into the realm of speculation. We have already mentioned the Emperor Constantine. Recent interpretations of church history have given him a bad press: the Monarch venerated as "apostle-like" by the ancient Church

---

1. The pope at the time of writing was Benedict XVI.

did not end the cruel persecution of Christians instituted by his predecessors simply because he had become a Christian in his heart once he had ascended to the throne—so the thinking goes—but rather in order to use the pertinacious Christian minority, growing ever larger in number of martyrs, to bolster a Roman Empire that had fallen into religious disorientation. Constantine used Christianity, it is said, to secure imperial power. By elevating the bishops—recently threatened with torture—to the status of prefects, he made the Church of the Nazarene into a state ideology. After one thousand and seven hundred years of Christian art and culture it is admittedly difficult to regret the decision of Constantine, regardless of its motives. Let us just muse on this matter, quite soberly and objectively: does it not seem that the Chinese Imperium is now in a similar situation to that of the Roman Empire after Diocletian? What if the Chinese leadership, in the face of the ideological crisis of the emerging superpower, entertained similar considerations as those that once confronted Constantine? After all, the small minority of Chinese Christians numbers 80 million faithful, with a large proportion of those being among the well-educated; there would be few purely card-carrying Christians among them. We should also remember that the truly effective missionary activity was overwhelmingly due to military activity or political pressure. With this in mind anyone could paint a picture of the consequences which a Catholic state Church in China would have for global politics: for the relationship of China to the West, particularly America; to Islam; whether it would produce the Westernization of the East, or rather the Easternization of the West; what changes would confront the global Church; what would become of the papacy if it were to amalgamate itself with the notion of the Emperor of China; what chance Beijing would have of becoming the Fourth Rome. The only weakness in this speculation is that it is real enough to be not entirely improbable. Only the unforeseeable, however, will step onto the stage of life.

Pope Without a Country

When I think of Pope Benedict XVI, the first thing which strikes me is his extremely idiosyncratic face: the large child's eyes that lie in shadowy caves and which appear to shine in expectation, even when he is sunk deep in thought. One sees such a face but rarely in his Bavarian homeland; the great novelist Heimito von Doderer said: "The Bavarian people is comprised of two groups; the smaller consists of butchers, the larger of people who look like butchers." The pope does not come across as particularly German. His politeness never deserts him and his placidity seems only to grow during controversial discussions, without him giving away an inch of ground. His movements are controlled: when he moves, he leans his upper body ever so slightly forward and glides as if on rails. One would be tempted to speak of the charm of Benedict XVI, if such a term were not rather too indiscreet and personal for him. His enemies call him cold, because he does not feign cordiality in the face of enemies—his etiquette is not influenced in any way by the lectures of Dale Carnegie. Attention and respect for the other are rarer and more valuable than the radiant features of some people's tribune. There is always a hint of melancholy in his smile. At his enthronement no burning hemp was held before his eyes as was once the custom while the words "Sic transit gloria mundi" (Latin: "So passes the glory of this world") were chanted; yet he is well aware of the limits of his actions. His speech is beautiful and this is strikingly conspicuous in a highly-placed German, for German is difficult and spoken well by only a very few Germans. Although he is a philosopher and a theologian, he has discovered a crystal-clear way of expressing himself, without simplifying the complicated subject matter he has to deal with. Is this not a virtue which befits a pastor?

Subversive Catholicism

In other nations it may have been noticed that official Catholicism in Germany greeted the spectacular election of a German as pope in a somewhat restrained manner, to put it mildly. German Catholicism is rich and very bourgeois. It enjoys significant state privileges and is afraid of overstepping the political and societal boundaries. German Bishops and prominent laity live in a constant state of anxiety; they worry that they might step out of line with the democratic consensus of an enlightened liberalism. It is as if they have forgotten that the Church is very old and that she has survived many societal systems and upheavals throughout history and that, in many centuries, she was not completely "up to date." Least so at the time of her foundation in late antiquity, in an urbanized, enlightened, multicultural, atomized and individualized society which, by a slow process, she permeated and transformed. Pope Benedict XVI may well be of the conviction that democracy has just as little right to meddle in the workings of the Church as many emperors and kings who attempted to do the same in earlier centuries. Unloved as he was among his German colleagues—they were intimidated by contemporary culture—he was fascinating to intellectuals who remain distant from the Church. Superficial reconciliatory rhetoric made no impression upon these circles; instead, in the person of Benedict XVI they experienced the authentic representative of a religion of which they knew nothing. Should they see it as "dangerous" or possibly as the only remaining alternative to secular society?

The election of a pope with the name of Benedict may certainly be taken as programmatical for the pontificate. Even as a cardinal the pope had fought against the tendency to see the Second Vatican Council as a "Super Council," with which the history of the Church was only beginning. "Benedict" reopened the profound depths of Church history, deep into the first Christian millennium when the Latin and Greek churches were still united. The grand Latin liturgy and Gregorian chant are particularly connected to the Benedictine Order. At his enthronement the pope once again wore the woolen pallium, such as the popes of the first millennium wore. He allowed the Gospel to again be proclaimed in Latin and Greek as was once common in every papal Mass. It is certain that, in the old liturgy, he sees a sign of the unity between East and West. His severity in questions of doctrine was certainly a response to the fact that, after the Second Vatican Council, ecclesial doctrine and liturgy lost some of its clarity. A restoration of the liturgy may well belong among the tasks of this pontificate, a restoration that primarily aims at reconciliation with the church in Byzantium. The amount of explosive material contained in this enterprise is shown by the words of Cardinal Ratzinger himself: the Orthodox Church should not be expected to acknowledge any greater degree of papal primacy than it accepted during the time of its unity with Rome.

    He who wishes to build bridges as the pontifex must first firm up his own shore. If the deceased pope placed "man in his God-given dignity" at the center of his teaching, Benedict could turn again to the nature of Jesus. The theology of the West has long since displayed signs of creeping Arianism. It is within the character of Pope Benedict, if he places his whole effort behind the attempt, to once again make the concept of the Incarnation of God comprehensible in a new language to the theologians, teachers, and intellectuals of modern civilization. Coming from the mouth of a man who is convinced that there is no contradiction between rationality and faith, this doctrine would sound as though there had never been any doubt about it.

He Is, After All, Only the Pope

Pope Benedict XVI described the hours before his election that brought him to the Chair of Peter in 2005, with the words: "I saw the guillotine approach me." No one knew better than he what would confront the new pope. No one surveyed the four decades that had passed since the end of the Second Vatican Council with greater accuracy than he. This council had claimed an exceptional status among the councils of Church history: while in the past a council had determined a theological point of contention which had arisen and inaugurated a phase of consolidation, the Second Vatican Council—which largely confirmed in its constitutions the inherited doctrine of the Church—opened a time of theological controversy, of uncertainty, of a loss of substance and of manifest breaks from tradition. It had wished to introduce an "opening to the world," yet after forty years it must be conceded that the Church is less able than ever before to make her quintessential concerns intelligible and that, despite her greatest assiduity in trying to reappropriate the secularized realm, she has lost the language needed to represent what is most specific to her. Theological chaos meant that in many nations no religious education worthy of the name took place; in Germany, Catholic Christianity has become an unknown religion even among Catholics. Some spoke of a revolution in the Church: her internal and external appearance had changed so radically that talk of "development" and "unfolding"—the preferred terms of ecclesiology—could no longer be maintained. Benedict XVI, however, was far from daunted by this gloomy state of affairs. Although he views the passage of time with an acute sense for history, for him the Church is not to be quantified in historical, sociological, or political terms. Benedict believes in the Church as articulated in the Credo, he believes in her being led by the Holy Spirit, and he believes in her ability to pick herself up again after a fall. For him the notion that the Church has undergone a revolution is an illusion—an illusion that some people welcome. As the Church of Jesus Christ is obliged to pass on that which she has received, there can be no revolution within her. Where there has been no revolution, however, there can also be no reaction. As pope, Benedict walks the path between revolution and reaction because he feels this is the path of the Church. This becomes particularly clear in his book on Jesus, which combines the insights of recent critical readings with the conviction that the martyrs of early Christianity did not die for a philological daydream. In the search for reconciliation with the Orthodox or the reconciliation of the politically divided Chinese Catholics he hazards risks that would not be possible for a conservative. Amidst the spiritual desiccation of the contemporary Church even a change in atmosphere can signify much. Why do none of our critical minds feel uncomfortable with the demand that the Church ought to subordinate herself totally to the present time and current conceptions of society? Why should there be a purely secular civil society that is entitled to prescribe the measure for everyone, including the Church? Viewed from the vantage point of Church history, the Church has always done poorly when she uncritically adapted herself to the spirit of the age. The pope may wish to protect the Church from a continuation of this dangerous state of affairs, for the sake of her own future.

Pope Pius X, the saintly promoter of Gregorian chant and of the traditional liturgy, was implored to include St. Joseph, the husband of Mary, within the canon of the Mass—that most exalted prayer in the Mass—among the long list of saints who had stood there since time immemorial. I couldn't do that, was Pius's answer: "I am, after all, only the pope." There is no better phrase than that to characterize the understanding Benedict XVI has of his office. He is, in his own understanding, "only the pope." Even as a cardinal he gave explanations of the dogma of infallibility that were far removed from naïve triumphalism and papal omnipotence: the infallibility accorded to papal determinations of dogma signifies nothing less than the subjection of the pope to tradition. Taking the name of Benedict upon his election, he probably liked the fact that, along with the associations which are bound up with that name, he would also be inheriting the high figure that made him the sixteenth Benedict; one in a row of many. For him, to be pope does not mean to invent anew the Church and the papacy, but rather to receive from the hands of his predecessors—in all humility—what their successor must hand on unharmed. For him, the pope does not belong among those who accomplish extraordinary acts, the political figures who are at home among tactical maneuvers and the preservation of power. The higher the papacy's aims, the more gently the pope ought to tread; his vision does not stretch toward the next election, but rather to a distant future. Something that today remains obscure may turn out to be a dependable foundation for this future. Benedict understands his task as that of a gardener who does everything he can to bring about fruit which neither he nor his contemporaries will enjoy. In a time characterized by profound uncertainty and lack of standards, the pope—who will not allow his agenda to be dictated by a daily press cycle hostile to the Church, but never loses sight of his long term goals—provokes a sense of indignation which occasionally becomes outright hatred. To "only be the pope," to be irrevocably bound to a law not created by himself: this is an unbearable source of irritation for a society that wants every value to be subject to fundamental revision.

    The moral scandal which has rocked the Church—above all in Germany and Ireland—which followed the discovery of a series of cases of abuse in the United States, was certainly the most important incident with which the pope had to deal at the time of the fifth anniversary of his election. Over the course of the passionately held discussions concerning this phenomenon it has become clear to all and sundry that, in cases of the abuse of children, we are concerned with crimes

Subversive Catholicism

that are pervasive throughout the whole of contemporary society and which are in no way particularly characteristic of the clergy of the Catholic Church. All the same, the pope himself understands these acts of individual priests as by far the worst symptom of the state of the Church which—in the time following the Second Vatican Council—fell into the path of the movement of '68 and threw overboard her identity, an identity which until then had been protected through all storms and seasons. It was the Old Testament itself that proclaimed the protection of children from sexual abuse in a world that had no qualms about erotic relationships with children. The protection of children is a genuine Christian message: a priest who offends against this message has thus not only broken his vows, but has also failed in his belief. For the Catholic Church, the scandal of abuse is the miserable apogee of postconciliar development; it is the most mortifying fruit of the ideology of *"aggiornamento"* (Italian: "bringing up to date") which shaped the past forty years. Although the council once more confirmed the inherited theology of the priesthood, little of it remained in the forty years that followed. Priests were urged to give up wearing their priestly garments; the obligation of daily celebrating Mass and praying the breviary was abolished; the sacredness of the priest's office was rejected. People forgot that the evangelical counsels called for poverty and obedience as well as chastity. In its essence the Catholic priesthood is a profoundly un-bourgeois institution, sharply opposed to the bourgeois values of autonomy and self-realization; yet this contradiction, above all else, was felt to be unbearable no longer simply by society, but also by the clergy and in particular the higher clergy. Every countermovement was futile so long as the *aggiornamento*-Church—represented in Germany by the long-time president of the Bishops' Conference, Cardinal Lehmann, and the functionaries of the Central Committee of German Catholics—could warm itself in the sun of society's approval; now that the intellectual and moral glamor of the *aggiornamento*-experiment has sunk into embarrassment, it will again be possible to recall the foundations of the Catholic priesthood and return to the principles that were handed down. While the pope labors under the wounds which the malefactors have inflicted upon the Church—certainly more than the hateful attacks upon his person, which copycat journalists connect with the scandal—he can be hopeful that his invitation to a renewal of the Catholic priesthood will be heard by the coming generation of priests. A positive sign was the Loyalty Address that former Cardinal Secretary of State Sodano gave at an unusual time, during the Easter Mass—an address in which he assured the pope of the fidelity of the clergy. Sodano had long since been an antagonist of Cardinal Ratzinger, a man of the "postconciliar process"; the point had arrived for old differences to be buried; this too may have given the pope hope for his next steps.

Reprimanding public opinion for its apparent lack of comprehension of the particularities of the Catholic Church does not help matters if we do not admit, at the same time, that it was the great lack of orientation within wide circles in the Church herself—circles that, in the decades following the Second Vatican Council, were not ready to examine their own priorities—that helped bring about this state of affairs. One cannot expect the laity (a laity that, often enough, does not even want to be Christian) to know more about the nature of the Catholic Church than the Church herself provides. Thus the crisis of postconciliar liturgy was seen, even by those who recognized the introduction of banality and a lack of tradition into liturgical celebrations and even deplored it, as a *peripheral problem* of merely aesthetic significance; what the liturgy itself truly means for the Church has largely been forgotten, even by Catholics. Even uninvolved observers must have pondered the fact that, until the intervention of Pope Paul VI, the Church had held fast to the inherited form of the liturgy throughout the many centuries of her existence. The profound, often catastrophic upheavals in history since late antiquity had given her no cause to change this liturgy that, right up to the present day, in its living celebration, enables us to experience the character of Christianity's founding age.

This fidelity to tradition is rooted in the knowledge that the *content* of the teachings of Jesus Christ cannot be separated from the *form*: the old formula *"lex orandi—lex credendi"* (Latin: "what we pray is what we believe") says nothing more than that the entire plenitude of Catholic faith, in its paradoxical complexity, is transformed through the liturgical celebration (that can be traced back to its origins) into a *visible event*. In the religion of the divine Incarnation there can be, in principle, no mere externalities. The physical, bodily performance of the liturgy is understood as pregnant with and saturated with meaning; therefore modifications or even new creations within the liturgical realm will always create interference in the body of doctrine as well. This is no theoretical claim, but rather proved a thousand times over by postconciliar experience. In the contemporary Church, core concepts such as sacrament and priesthood are often obscured to the point of being unrecognizable.

Pope Benedict has long since been aware of this vital danger for the Church. The Church is not some political party, which can throw ideological ballast overboard when it is no longer opportune for the preservation of its power. Her goal is universality, but not at the price of her obligation to the truth. If this truth is no longer acceptable to the majority, more the pity for that majority. At the same time, he sees his task as mitigating those theological unrests of the past decades, thereby seeking to avoid an abrupt change of course. His strong historical sense recognizes in the false developments, which he diagnoses, not only personal fault and the failure of those responsible, but also the powerful influence of a mentality typical of our times and that cannot be tackled by commands. The healing of the wounds which have been inflicted by unrest within the Church can only occur gradually; "patience" is one of the most important words of this pope, who accepts being misunderstood by friend and foe alike and has faith in the gradual unfolding of his thoughts in the future.

He Is, After All, Only the Pope

A decisive role in the rescue of the liturgy fell to the Society of St Pius X, a rebellious group of priests surrounding the French Archbishop Lefebvre. The bishops of this society were ordained contrary to the ban of Pope John Paul II and found themselves in the state of excommunication. Pope Benedict lifted the proscription of the traditional liturgy and announced that it had never been in the Church's power to forbid it. Rescuing the traditional liturgy also involved reconciliation with the five hundred priests of this society, who in their fight for the sake of the liturgy—now declared justified by the pope—had endured grievous suffering and disadvantage. Furthermore, in the isolation of expulsion they had developed in ways which were theologically and politically alarming. Conscious of the responsibility which the Church bore for each one of the priests of St. Pius X, the pope ventured a decision of unique courage, unintentionally provoking the lack of comprehension of a public that was by now alienated from Catholic tradition: in priestly generosity he ended the dangerous state of expulsion of these overwhelmingly young priests and placed his trust in rapprochement in the spirit of patient and respectful efforts at persuasion, and in an open theological discussion. As far as the media were concerned, the scandal of these events hid the historic ecclesial dimension of the papal decision. One of the bishops freed from excommunication, the Englishman Williamson—feared as a vain eccentric within his own society—appeared on television as a Holocaust denier. Because the Vatican press spokesman had not thought it necessary to enlighten the public as to the spiritual character of a ban of excommunication and its subsequent lifting, the impression was given that the pope wished to rehabilitate the political lunacy of this bishop. The opposite was generally known to be the case. Yet even if the "slip-up"—as the pope called the failure of the press spokesman—had not occurred, must we not conclude that the theological illiteracy of even the Catholic journalists, after four postconciliar decades, had obstructed Benedict's intentions? Should Benedict's pontificate have been left hostage to a man whose views he deplored? The first fruit of the papal decision was that the Society of St. Pius finally succeeded in removing Williamson from its executive committee. The unification talks with the Society of St. Pius are proceeding in the calm and spiritual earnestness which is appropriate to the treatment of theological problems. It seems that a reconciliation with the society is no longer without prospects. And, at the same time, younger priests in many places within the Catholic world are discovering a new sense of the meaning of the liturgy and its connection to the great sacramental tradition of the Church. They are not changes which make headlines; it is a gradual, almost imperceptible change in thinking—this is exactly the manner that lies close to the pope's own heart; an almost silent change of heart, an organic development.

According to an ancient formula, the pope is named on all official documents—regardless of whether he found himself in greatest distress or whether the historical hour was favorable to him—"*feliciter regnans*," happily reigning. It could seem as though this formula, applied to Benedict XVI, has an ironic or even bitter aftertaste. Can this phrase apply to a man who, with each of his pronouncements, unleashes misinterpretation? The first pope since Peter to undertake an attempt to read the New Testament with the eyes of a Jew—and yet he is constantly accused of being an anti-Semite? The man who, in his Regensburg Address, initiated the first truly profound and extremely fruitful dialogue of the Catholic Church with Islam, and is instead found guilty of having destroyed this relationship with Islam? The man who condemns the abuse of children by priests with such severity that it seems he has forgotten Christian compassion for the sinner, and yet is reviled and accused of having covered up the malefactors? The opposite of happiness is misfortune. Is Pope Benedict simply unfortunate? Are his aides not able to "sell" the pope more effectively, as the phrase goes (which suggests that with the appropriately sleazy methods anything could be launched onto the market)? This impression could arise with this or that individual case, but taking everything together it becomes clear: no, "misfortune" is the wrong word for this pope. Naturally the memory of the public successes of his predecessor, the heart-conquering John Paul II, stands before us. He led the Church to a presence in the world that is comparable only with the effect of the medieval popes. Yet it is no secret that, behind a gleaming façade, the Church's internal condition had long since been in peril. The spiritual erosion had reached critical mass. Would it be very cynical to suggest that such a Church was just what many of her enemies wanted? A Church that was on the point of losing her religious force, her otherness, her sacredness: one could cope with such a Church; the old (but still applicable) motto of Voltaire "Écrasez l'infâme" (French: "Crush the loathsome thing!"— i.e., the Church) could be laid aside for a while. With Benedict one senses a return to the Church's almost forgotten claim to truth: it is becoming clear that the pope is serious in his fight against relativism, and that he wants Catholics to be Catholic once again. An influential portion of public opinion recognizes that this is a declaration of war. Their response is: the pope must not be allowed to put a foot on the ground. If he were a politician, he ought to be nervous. But the strength of this gentle and cautious man—who himself rejects the use of the instruments of power—lies in the very fact that he is not a politician. He has recognized his mission, he is the only one who can fulfil it, he is in the right place to do so—is that not a "happy" conjunction? And that is why Benedict XVI is also, in the fullest sense of the words, a pope "happily reigning."

On the Pope

I

WAS PETER ACTUALLY in Rome? Did he die on a cross in Rome, or somewhere else in his bed? Is Saint Peter's, with Bernini's gigantic bronze tabernacle, actually built over the grave of St. Peter? These are new questions: it has taken the last century—a century that has put a question-mark over everything traditionally held—to formulate them. One of the favorite peculiarities of what we call the "Enlightenment" is a certain predilection for conspiracy theories. Charlemagne, for instance, never existed, along with the three centuries that were supposed to have followed him: they originated in cunning forgeries made by clergy of the Ottonian dynasty. Shakespeare is not Shakespeare but Francis Bacon or the Earl of Oxford. And as for Peter's death in Rome, it is a priests' invention, providing substance for the papacy's jurisdictional claims. But why, in all the centuries in which the primacy of the Bishop of Rome—as the successor of St. Peter—gradually unfolded, as from a seed, was the fact of Peter's grave in Rome never disputed? Why did Byzantine Orthodoxy—which had been engaged in a bitter power struggle with the Roman pope since well before the split between the Western Church and the Eastern—never question Peter's martyr's death in Rome and his "primacy of honor" among the Church's patriarchs? The early Church was plagued by warring sects; every imaginable heresy was developed and proclaimed, so that one can say, with all accuracy, that there has never been a theological controversy since that time that did not have roots in these first centuries—but all early Christians accepted that Peter, as Bishop of Rome, was crucified under the emperor Nero. There may be no entry in the city of Rome population registry; there may be no certificate of execution; but the Galilean fisherman who came to the city left traces behind him, primarily in the memories of those people who became Christians because of his preaching.

Trusting tradition is a central feature of the Catholic Church. For a Catholic there is something slightly irritating about having to adopt the pseudo-scientific rituals of the present time and having to cite the most up-to-date researches that confirm what he already knew, i.e., that Peter founded the Roman Church.

"God needed two things in order to become man: the womb of the Virgin and the Latin language." Paul Claudel's dictum—provocative, as one would expect of this writer—sums up how a Catholic sees world history. The Word became flesh "in the fullness of time" and, more particularly, in a province of the Roman Empire: so this supernatural event was most closely associated with Rome. If the Church were to survive, if faith in Jesus Christ were to be transmitted to future generations, an institution to ensure this was necessary, and the institution par excellence was the Roman state that, under the emperors, was developing into a universal monarchy. Given this basic state of affairs, the theological debate about the degree of the pope's jurisdiction that is essential to the exercise of the papal office, and how much of this was subsequently usurped (or even contradicted the original form of the papal office), is actually superfluous.

Initially, of course, the papacy rested on Jesus's multifaceted word concerning the "rock on which I will build my Church" and on the command of Jesus to "feed my sheep" and to "confirm your brothers in the faith." These utterances do not mean that we can automatically deduce from them the whole of Roman centralism as it developed especially in the second millennium. Nonetheless, the locating of Peter's office in Rome indicated the path along which this office, emerging from the catacombs, gradually unfolded as the administration of a worldwide Church. It was providential; it simply had to be. The doctrine of the two natures of Christ, human and divine, produced a similar "two natures" view of the Church: there was the divine institution, sinless and eternal; and there was the Church embodied not only in the pope but in all the baptized—human and subject to human failings—a view that cannot be separated from its Latin and juristic spirit.

Accordingly the apogee of the papacy's development—the dogma of papal infallibility in matters of faith and morals, pronounced in 1871 at the first Vatican Council, following the loss of the Papal States—did not result in some absolutist empowering of the papacy (as it was erroneously seen) but in the expression of its constitution: the pope was explicitly subordinated to the whole tradition of the Church. What is infallible is not a person but the great body of two thousand years' tradition in scripture, word and customs—of which the pope currently reigning is only the mouthpiece.

What of the future of the papal office? Who would dare to be a prophet in this matter? Jesus's promise that "the gates of hell shall not prevail" against the Rock does not imply that the Church will reach the end of the ages in splendor and amplitude—elsewhere his view of the future seems to imply the opposite. The anthropologist Arnold Gehlen (d. 1976) expressed his conviction that "the Christian age is over." Indications for Europe may suggest this, but what of the—very substantial—rest of the world? Standing by the catafalque of Pius IX, Gregorovius (1821–1891) the historian of Rome observed that the pope "is lying there like a fallen idol," the "last representative of the political papacy"—and then John Paul II arrived and became the most politically influential pope in the whole of Church history since Innocent III. To realize the future potential of the papacy, even today, one has only to imagine what would happen if, at the next Conclave, the cardinals were to elect as pope a Chinese man who had spent twenty years in a Chinese concentration camp. It would be reminiscent of the time when Emperor Constantine brought the persecuted bishops out of their hideouts. Anyone who observes our world as it is at present can paint his own picture of the consequences of such an election—it would change the face of the world.

Subversive Catholicism

II

In Rome the papal institutions are termed *sacer,* literally translated as "holy, sacred." Thus a papal ministry, for instance, is called a "sacred congregation." This image was adopted from the Roman emperors: for them *sacer* meant nothing other than "imperial." It was a word that asserted the immunity and untouchable nature of the highest organs of state. In fact, in the long centuries since Peter, the popes were anything but "untouchable": there were few periods when the papal office was not exposed to the most virulent attacks. In their hieratic remoteness many popes seemed like European pendants for the priest-like Chinese emperors—this image evokes the battles and menaces, sometimes highly physical, against which, during the course of its history, the papacy had to stand fast.

The first followers of Peter died martyrs' deaths like himself. Under Roman emperors—some of them Christian—popes were deposed and banished. In the early Middle Ages the body of a pope was tipped from its coffin into the Tiber by an enraged populace; another pope's corpse was made the subject of a formal trial and ultimately desecrated. popes had to flee, were driven out and had to seek refuge. Boniface XIII's ears were boxed by the French king's ambassador; and the papacy was placed under French tutelage in Avignon. Anti-popes were elected, and one pope was deposed by the Council of Constance. At the Sack of Rome the pope had to watch from the parapets of the Fortress of St. Angelo as the emperor's army devastated Rome in the worst plundering of all time. Christian princes—not only Protestant ones—renounced their allegiance to the papacy. Pius VI and Pius VII were dragged from Rome and kept in isolation on French territory. The Church State—the oldest European state—was conquered and broken up. And in the twentieth century a tank stood in front of the Vatican with its muzzle pointing toward St. Peter's Basilica, while German army officials deliberated whether it would not be better to take the pope into custody. Paul VI and John Paul II were subject to life-threatening attacks.

More danger was involved, perhaps, in the case of the many popes who did not measure up to their high office. Some were bad priests and weak rulers; some were greedy power-politicians, some were fettered by their own family interests, others were limited and blind when it came to the demands of the particular historical moment. How could an institution subject to so many different attacks survive multiple dramatic historical upheavals when, in crises, its head was so often ineffective?

In all this an atheist might see the machinations of a worldwide plot to oppress whole peoples. A sociologist, perhaps, would point to the power of an institution that is more than the sum of its members and stronger than its individual office-bearers. A traditional Protestant could recall Luther's condemnation of the papal Whore of Babylon, which will only be destroyed at the Last Judgment. A cynical agnostic might blame the stupid populace, unteachable, clinging to paternalistic authority against all reason. As for the Catholic, he would have to insist that the pope is not the Church's head at all, but only the latter's representative or "stand-in" and, as such, not ultimately responsible for the success and good fortune of the historical Church.

III

Even those hostile to the papacy would have to admire the shape and construction of this office that, from the beginning, has preserved it—in the person of Peter—from crises. As the successor and representative of Christ, as the Rock on which the Church is to be built, even the most capable office-bearer is bound to fail. For this office of "confirming his brothers in faith" Christ chose the very disciple who, while he had always shown courage and vitality, failed when it came to acknowledging his Master. "Then he began to curse and swear"—the evangelist, describing Peter's apostasy beside the fire in the

Subversive Catholicism

High Priest's courtyard, leaves us in no doubt as to the seriousness of this betrayal.

By choosing Peter, Christ shows that the office of representative requires no special intellectual gifts and talents, no firmness of character, and no proven stability—which means that every man is equally fitted and unfitted for this office. Christ became man and therefore every man is equally equipped to represent him. No pope can betray Christ more than Peter did in that courtyard, no pope can follow Christ more than Peter, who had himself crucified on his account. The choice of Peter establishes the clear distinction, in the Church, between the office and the person. It is this principle that makes it possible to encounter the incarnate, grace-bestowing Christ even in unworthy human beings. The choice of Peter also makes concrete the Catholic anthropology that sees man as weak and sinful, and yet called to pursue the highest perfection. The choice of Peter established a fundamental disjunction between the Church and its earthly and political success, making it resistant to disappointment in the face of its historical achievement.

The office established in the person of Peter was equally effective in world leadership and in underground operations. As Carl Schmitt (German political theorist, d. 1985) wrote, mocking the *aggiornamento* ("bringing up to date") that followed the Second Vatican Council:

> "Go with the flow," Heraclitus teaches;
> —and Peter's Rock the same thing preaches.

This Rock, however, has been both firm and fluid in all centuries and has been able to adapt itself to the most diverse political milieu: in early times the pope was a Roman state official, and in the Middle Ages he was a Germanic feudal lord. At one time he was a Baroque sovereign, and in the nineteenth century civil wars he represented the anti-revolutionary party. In the twentieth century, having lost the Papal States and being liberated from the chains of Italian national politics, he became the head of a global NGO. Nor can we envisage any end to these transformations, for the great ideas of modern times (that were potentially dangerous for the papacy) have all imploded. Perhaps the Catholic Church really does have the key to the mystery of her invincible form of government?

It is sometimes more productive, in engaging in a critique of some institution, to ask about its ideal realization rather than its mistakes. Mistakes are there, everywhere and all the time. There have been moments in history—not seldom either—when the papacy presented an overwhelming picture of wisdom and beauty, and exhibited a wealth of culture—completely infused with spirituality—in which it seemed possible to combine goodness, gentility, and beauty with power, in a way that would last. But in that case, where was the "vale of tears" that, according to Christian conviction, characterizes the earth? A papacy that, according to its own ideas, had "succeeded"—some kind of paradise on earth—would not this be an impossibility for Christianity? The legitimate goal of completely saturating the world sacramentally, of materializing the Spirit in a beautiful world order, contains a certain danger: it might cause us to forget the "yonder world," as if the Last Judgment were already behind us. Such a danger is purely theoretical, however: the reality of the "vale of tears" is always quick to show itself once more.

IV

That Emperor Constantine the Great had not only built three impressive basilicas in Rome—the Lateran basilica as the church of the Bishop of Rome and St. Peter's and St. Paul's over the graves of these princes of the apostles—and handed over to Pope Sylvester the imperial Palace of the Lateran, but had also given him in addition the land around Rome as a Church State: this "Donation of Constantine" had already been shown, in the Middle Ages, to be a naïve forgery. It could just as well be described as a fairy-tale (albeit with a true core, as fairy-tales often have). Constantine founded his new city of Constantinople and, together with all his senators, abandoned Rome, whereas the pope remained behind in the former imperial palace, refusing to become the all-powerful emperor's court chaplain.

By leaving Pope Sylvester in Rome, Constantine *did* present him with Rome, metaphorically speaking; for this event initiated the popes' freedom and their acquisition of Rome—even though, formally, the city remained under imperial authority. It was the Franks, however, who first created a special kingdom for the pope, because according to the Germanic law on fiefdom, ownership of land was always connected with lordship. From now on, the representative of Him whose "kingdom is not of this world" possessed an empire of his own in this world.

There was never a time when the popes' worldly power was not criticized. Not only did the emperor's lawyers insist that the Church ought to be poor and that the Vicar of the Crucified should be powerless in this world (for the emperor wanted to subordinate the pope to himself), but the same view was put forward by the many medieval popular movements of "the poor." Even the resounding voice of medieval Christian culture, Dante Alighieri, called for a papacy stripped of all property. Particularly during Dante's lifetime, however, when the popes had come under the thumb of the French king and were obliged to do his will, there was a clear spiritual advantage in having an independent papacy with its own state. By the time of the Avignon papacy, at least, it became obvious that the Catholic Church, embracing all countries in the world, needed a territory in which the pope was no man's subject and no republic's citizen, and was removed as far as is possible on this earth from the grasp of the mighty. The measure of politics is the gradual, not the ideal solution.

Since that time Catholics have two fatherlands (or motherlands): their own, and the Roman Church State, which, by the twentieth century, had shrunk to a manageable size. Whether ultramontane or ultramarine, beyond the mountains or beyond the seas, part of a Catholic's loyalty is reserved to the pope—and the mistrustful anti-Catholic propaganda, even in the twentieth century, asserted that this loyalty to the pope was the more significant.

This division of loyalty, however, was one of the most important presuppositions of European freedom. The struggle of monarch against pope for the obedience (and the cash) of their subjects resulted in the latter's freedom—not that it was deliberately intended by the former. The fact that the pope appealed to the conscience of Christians, over the heads of the national rulers, prevented the creation of a *societas perfecta*, a self-sufficient, self-enclosed society, which in the twentieth century was called a "totalitarian state." The Church's direct dependence on (even) a benevolent state is troubling enough, but the twentieth century produced the criminal state. Even those Greek, Bulgarian, Serbian, and Russian Orthodox who only grant the papal primacy as a primacy of honor, and reject his involvement with national churches, will admit that the extraterritorial status of the Church's highest bishop can protect him from getting implicated in the policies of an evil regime. We see this in the pontificate of John Paul II, who was lifted out of the power of the Soviet regime and placed on the *Cathedra Petri* ("the Chair of Peter"). If the Donation of Constantine did not exist, it would more than shrewd, it would be *wisdom* to invent it.

V

One of world history's most astonishing dramas is the transformation of a world monarchy into a world Church. Jesus Christ was born a son of the most nationalist of all nations and a subject of an empire that claimed to be universal. The emperors under whose rule he was born and crucified are named in the New Testament. Of a Roman soldier he once said that "he had not found such great faith in Israel." The

Subversive Catholicism

goal of Peter's and Paul's great missionary journeys was Rome. Subsequently, however, the image of Rome darkened in the early age of Christendom. The city and the empire it exemplified became the epitome of evil; it became the Babylon of John's arcane Book of Revelation, and Roman rule became a symbol of injustice, of the triumph of the "Beast" that precedes the end of the world. Still, the centuries that came before the great change under Constantine did not by any means represent an uninterrupted persecution of Christians; between Nero and Diocletian there were ever longer periods of peaceful coexistence in which the Church could expand, developing and establishing its episcopal structure.

Then came the unimaginable, unpredictable moment in history when Emperor Constantine elevated the bishops, many of whom still bore scars and mutilations from Diocletian's torturers, to the rank of imperial prefects. From then on the Church gradually grew and inserted itself into the institutions of the Roman empire, until it had completely occupied and absorbed them.

Since the end of the eighteenth century it became customary to speak of the Fall of the Roman empire. Up to that time specialists in state law had considered the Roman empire to be not at all defunct, but a continuing entity. But even if, from today's vantage-point, we do not consider the European nations' statehoods and national configurations (in the wake of the *Völkerwanderung*, the "migration of peoples") to be simply a continuation of the Roman empire, its continuance in the form of the Roman Church is plain to see. Goethe, in his *Zahme Xenien*, created a formula of unique precision for this phenomenon in a dialogue between Jesus and the city of Rome:

> JESUS: And shall our pact endure, through ages all the same?
> ROME: *Rome* now I'm called; *Humanity*, then, will be my name.

A universal idea of civilization had become a religious idea of humanity.

It is historically characteristic of the Roman Church that she keeps faith with the different stages she has gone through in her history. She does not feel the individual phases of her development as something left behind, something that has been overcome, but as the necessary precondition for her present and future. This is illustrated whenever the pope—or, for that matter, any bishop—celebrates a solemn pontifical liturgy: underneath his priestly chasuble he wears the vestments corresponding to the inferior grades of consecration (deacon, subdeacon). For the Church of Rome, being united with its past is not an intellectual principle: it is a theology that is experienced by the senses. Its authority consists in its claim to make present the Son of God who appeared on earth at a particular time in world history: it renders the past present, so that we may reach the concrete (not mythical) Jesus of Nazareth. The carpenter's son lived in freely-chosen poverty, but this visible aspect of his existence did not embrace the full truth about him: according to his own testimony and according to the belief of Christians he shared, at the same time, in God's glory.

When the popes took over, piece by piece, the insignia and forms of the Roman empire, they found an aesthetic and political language in which to make visible the truth of the glorified Christ, the King. More and more it seemed that ancient, imperial Rome, with its constitution that mingled republican and monarchical elements, had been only a preparation for the Church. The ceremonies of reverence that had been created for the emperor now applied to Jesus Christ, and only in this context did they become meaningful and justified. What had been glimpsed by Jesus's contemporaries during those few moments of the Transfiguration and the appearances of the Risen One—the glory of his true nature and the presence of the kingdom of God—believers were now to begin to grasp in the imperial splendor of the popes.

The Roman Church does indeed preserve the essential institutions of the Roman empire. The pope takes the place of the emperor, including his priestly title of *Pontifex maximus* ("the supreme bridge-builder"). He wears the red shoes of the emperor, which originated with the Roman republic's "sacrificial kings" (*rex sacrorum* was the title of the senator who presented the sacrificial gifts in ancient Rome); like Diocletian he is accompanied in liturgical processions by acolytes bearing candles and incense; he is surrounded by senators (the cardinals, who are clad in senatorial purple); and he receives the acclamation of the assembled people on the square of St. Peter's. A detailed examination will show innumerable instances of this continuity. Such instances have always attracted criticism. The amalgamation of Jesus's message of love with the Roman power-apparatus; the establishment of a priestly kingship that is supposed to represent the Crucified—these things have again and again been felt to be a mutation of Christianity into its opposite. Nonetheless the Catholic Church has held fast in this matter, and with good reason.

Things that are contradictory are fatal to all philosophical systems; for the Church, however, they constitute the rhythm of her thought. One could even say that thinking in paradoxes is the mystery of her vitality. In the dispute about the nature of Christ she withstood the clear, logically acceptable proposals of the Arians, who understood Christ to be God's creature, and of the Monophysites, who regarded him as an exclusively divine being, and instead came up with the impregnable formula "Christ is wholly man and wholly God."

God's enfleshment created the visible Church. The incarnate God wanted to be represented ("presented") by human beings. The kingdom of God on earth, however, is marred by the constant presence of original sin; the pendulum between the perfection of God's creation and the imperfection of the fallen world will not come to rest; through Christ the Redemption is made tangible, yet not totally. Through the Incarnation God has renewed man's dignity; the world and its matter is again made receptive to divinity, but men do not cease inflicting damage on this renewed status. The world hovers in a situation of continued sin and continued forgiveness. The human icon of this condition is the pope: he is the ruler of the empire of the Not-Yet. The fallen world needs order and forgiveness, and the pope stands for them both. He is a head of state, guaranteeing—through the millennia—the authenticity of the Christ-event, securing it against arbitrary subjectivism; and he is a priest, enabling the forgiveness of sins by making his Master present.

PART II

Liturgy in the Church

Prayer

Praying and Dying

"If God exists, then prayer is the only reasonable act," says Nicolás Gómez Dávila, and one could elaborate: if God does not exist, then prayer is in fact unreasonable; yet that would be immaterial, because in that case nothing whatsoever would be reasonable. Most of those who pray are not engaged in such considerations; they pray whether it is reasonable or not, even if it is the prayer of Henri Bergson: "Dear God, I thank you for not existing." As the saying goes, there are no atheists in an airplane plunging to disaster. And the question of a particular form does not arise when the briefest of prayers is all that is possible. The urge to pray gets by without theology. It can be silenced for a time in societies—like those of the contemporary West—exhibiting complex structures that deeply engross the individual person, but in most cases the urge to pray surfaces again when it comes to dying. To learn to pray means to learn to die. When death approaches—life's only certainty—we encounter reality; and for many it is possibly for the first time. There is widespread scorn for the many "free thinkers" and atheists who turn to a positive religion on their deathbed. Yet this scorn fails to understand the experience of feeling oneself, for the first time in one's life, completely powerless in the presence of another powerful will. In the realm that hovers between life and death, insights occur that go beyond belief, opinion, and conviction. The veil that covers reality is lifted but for a moment. That was why, in the old Catholic liturgy of the last rites, the feet of the dying were anointed: so that, should they survive the crisis, they might never walk again upon the earth in their old attitude, but rather hold fast to what they had experienced at the hour of death.

Subversive Catholicism

The most profound difference between the ancient cultures and the world of the contemporary West is perhaps the former's ability to be clear on the realities of life. Man must die and man must pray. To prepare for death is difficult, for it often comes unexpectedly. Prayer, on the other hand, can be practiced. This practice occurred, in every ancient culture, through the learning and mastery of rituals: while we are still in the realm of illusion we find ourselves unable to pray; but this inability is overcome by ritual. The throes and pains of death are usually the result of a will that strains against it. In ritual we learn to subject ourselves, in this most important aspect of our existence, to a foreign will, a pre-existing form. In ritual the truth—that man is not free but rather is handed over to an external will—becomes visible. It is one of the unsearchable paradoxes of feeling that the perception of a truth, even if it is a frightening one, is experienced as a relief.

It does not go easily with ritual in our present time. Even priests—whose only justification for existence is in the execution of rites—growl about "empty rituals," or "formalism that is remote from life," of "rigid ceremonies that seem to mean nothing to the people of today." One of the most important characteristics of a serviceable rite—namely, that it is ancient and that its origin cannot be precisely dated—is today held against it as a particular drawback.

Rites generally have a hierarchical structure: they cannot be carried out by just anyone, but they are there for all; they are the opposite of a spiritual class system. The rite is formed with the normal human being in mind; anyone who does not count himself among these is excused. Not only the irreligious but also the religious person elevates himself only seldom and with effort to the high level of his convictions and beliefs. Rites were created for egoistic, bigoted, superficial, ordinary people lacking in concentration. It is of the nature of a rite that something practiced unthinkingly by hundreds of people together creates an effect that far exceeds the intentions of the participants. The rite achieves more than would be possible by the spiritual efforts of the individual. The rite produces something which, for the individual man—even the most pious—is unattainable; and for that reason it belongs to the definition of a rite that it is not sustained by the spiritual powers of those who celebrate it. However, because the rite is more powerful than the abilities of those who celebrate it, the participants experience it—by performing it—as something that is independent of them. This effect is well known in art: the completed artwork often appears to the artist as if it were not made by him, as though the piece exceeds the artist's abilities. It has become both more and other than he was in a position to plan. In the ritual of praying, however, every man can become an artist. Thus it is a precondition of the rite that God is encountered as extrinsic to oneself, as something sundered from one's own soul, independent of it, bigger than it, even existent without it. In the ritual, the one who prays places himself under God's radiant sun, as depicted in the reliefs from the time of Akhenaten, in which the family of the king appears to be lovingly caressed by the little hands that terminate the sun's rays. Ritual allows the person praying to be active. Yet at the same time it allows him to forget his own capability and experience it as something worked by another hand; thus he can attain that prayer which Tersteegen describes as "Beholding God and allowing oneself to be beheld by Him."

The Churchy Type and "Pius Aeneas"

The attitude which favors prayer is called piety. Piety is a word that is now used only contemptuously or bashfully, even by priests and theologians. The churchy types are pious; people who, together with the parlor maid, have disappeared from reality yet are still utilized as social paradigms by people who have never encountered either the one or the other in their natural environment. Even believers superciliously assure one another that they are not, of course, pious. To be pious is

Subversive Catholicism

worse than to be stupid, attaching many other unattractive characteristics to stupidity: backwardness, awkwardness, being excessively self-effacing and inhibited. Which historical development it was that finally led our contemporaries to have such associations with the word "piety" can be left unmentioned. It is more worthwhile to recall what piety once actually meant. In the face of modern connotations of the word, is it not strange to hear that the Romans regarded their heroic founding father as pious?

Aeneas, leader of men, lover, battle-chieftain, was known among them, above all, for his *pietas*. It would be a mistake to regard the adjective "pious" as a mere ornament which accompanies Aeneas in all his activities in Virgil's poem, whether the son of Venus is kissing or abandoning the lovestruck Dido, whether he is drawing his sword or concluding a crafty treaty. Virgil was himself pious and he was convinced that all the heroic virtues and all the charm with which he characterized his heroes sprang from the general virtue of piety.

This piety is an expression of the conviction that, with every step and every action, we are observed by the gods. This conviction grows as, from the experience of chaos and senseless destruction, the structure of an initially mysterious and then ever-more clearly apparent plan begins to take shape. For the impious, the piety of Aeneas is a combination of dysfunctional relationships and a superiority complex: to believe in all earnestness that the entire universe could turn on one, solitary, poor human being in all of his inconsequentiality and meaninglessness! But the pious man indeed believes precisely that. He raises his hands to heaven and counts on the fact that a large ear bends down from heaven to hear him—and at the same time he must also anticipate—and approve of—the fact that millions and billions do the same and wish to find the self-same ear; and possibly even do find it. If one were to think of the chain-reactions that even the tiniest intervention in people's lives would initiate, the possibility that a supra-earthly authority is ceaselessly engaged in hearing the prayers of an uncounted mass of humanity—everywhere stiffening swords in mid-thrust and stopping mountains in mid-collapse—amounts almost to a terrifying fantasy. He who prays trusts in a higher order, runs the phrase, yet in truth he trusts equally in a ceaseless disruption and suspension of every form of reasonable order: he believes that the highest good, and what is *utterly* reasonable, is prepared—at the mere request of unreasonable and by no means good miniature monads—to abandon all necessity and order. To be pious is to be convinced that everything depends on each life, particular one's own. In the old baptismal rite of the Catholic Church, with its three great banishments of the devil, we are given the clearest possible picture of the world and of our own existence—as seen by the pious man. There lies the innocently blubbering infant amid his white pillows, while above his head there rages a spiritual battle in which armies of angels and demons are engaged in a battle for this tender, barely awoken soul. The pious man sees himself as a chess piece pushed hither and thither by some great power, taking steps on his own initiative in the field of operations—often unaware of it—steps that will determine whether he remains upon the board or leaves it. The pious man sees his life as a match between power and powerlessness, in which the superior power anxiously waits to see if the powerless party will make the correct decision. One can see that the pious man's view of the world, of nature and supernature, is incomparably bizarre. It is thus all the more surprising that this has been the view of the greater proportion of humanity throughout all epochs, including the present, and that it requires extraordinary spiritual resources to truly liberate oneself from it, with all its attendant consequences for daily life. Curiously and paradoxically, people who achieve this are called—insane.

Subversive Catholicism

The Necessity of Prayer Wheels

In Tibet there stand the enormous inverted bowls of the Stupas, around which the pilgrims walk; across the world and in almost every culture there is a holy space venerated by walking around it. These Stupas are surrounded by brass prayer wheels decorated with small flags, which the pilgrims brush up against in passing and thus cause to spin; within the casing there lie strips of parchment with prayers. The prayer wheel is an utter horror for modern Western theologians. For them, it is a caricature of ritual prayer, a grotesque symbol of empty spirituality and superficiality. At the same time, Christianity is also acquainted with prayer wheels, prayer machines, soulless material that is brought to prayer. In first place come the bells. People say that bells were always for calling people to prayer; bells, they say, do not pray. It will not do, however, to regard the ringing of bells as the prayer of the bell-ringer himself—although the sight of a man, bell rope in hand, bending his knees as he puts his entire weight on the rope, and then being lifted up into the air by the weight of the bell, could absolutely lead one to think of the work of prayer. Yet anyone who hears the ringing of bells knows that a mere signal, a mere call—plausible as it sounds—could never provoke as unique an effect as the bells do. Those who hear bells in a large city today will likely not know—unlike the farmers of yesteryear—precisely what liturgical time of prayer they indicate, nor will they feel themselves called to prayer. Nowadays, the ringing of the Angelus at midday and six in the evening—which even some Protestant churches maintain—leads so few faithful to pray that one must say that the Angelus prayer itself has indeed been completely taken over by the bells.

And this notion can without difficulty be brought into harmony with the doctrine of Christian prayer. It is precisely the ringing of bells at particular hours that confirms their independent meaning, unrelated to human activity.

According to the ancient Jewish and Christian view, the mere existence of the soulless world is already prayer, particularly the passing of time, the rising and setting of the sun, the change from day into night. After every Mass a Catholic priest is to pray privately the famous "Canticle of the three youths in the fire" from the Book of Daniel, in order to experience that the Mass he has just celebrated is integrated into the liturgy of the cosmos. The youths Ananias, Azarias, and Misael, who were meant to be burned yet, as a result of their prayer, remained unharmed in the flames, commanded the fire and the heat surrounding them to pray to God and praise Him; they describe rain, dew, frost, and snow as praying; lightning and thunder also pray, as do the springs, streams, and seas; birds, fish, wild and domestic animals pray too, and the prayer of man only falls into line with this general cosmic prayer; human prayer is a joining in, an addition to a celebration which had already begun, regardless. Because every existence provides a witness to the will of God, without whom it would not exist, every existence is praise of God. The Catholic view of the world is an expression of a sacral materialism. All material is created for the praise of God; some materials, however, in a quasi-priestly way, are especially so created. Water, from the beginning, was destined to be the instrument and body of the Holy Spirit; the bees—as tiny priestesses—create the wax for votive candles, and the fermentation of grape juice into wine predestines it, from the beginning of all time, to be the material of ritual transformation in the sacrifice of the Mass. Thus the ore of the bells was created in order to celebrate the ceaseless continuation of the cosmic sacrificial feast. The bells are messengers of prayer to the inanimate objects that merely exist.

"Oculis levatis ad caelum"

On a trip to the mainland a Friesian woman fell out of the boat; she almost drowned. "Did you pray," she was asked. "No, I couldn't," she answered, "I was holding onto my purse."

Subversive Catholicism

Necessity may know no laws, but the woman was essentially correct. Certain prayer-actions make it physically obvious that someone is praying: they are constituent elements of prayer, and occasionally even the prayer itself. The woman was prevented from bringing her hands together which, in the West, one can do in one of two ways: either by laying the palms of the hands against one another, as in Dürer's "Praying Hands," or by intertwining the fingers of the one hand with the other. Both gestures can be related to ancient feudal customs. The intertwined hands showed, it is said, that one did not intend to touch one's weapon; the hands pressed against one another were once placed by a knight between the hands of the lord to whom he swore allegiance. Yet the Egyptian Copts, who knew no knights, exchange the sign of peace in their liturgy in precisely the same manner, for all gestures that come to be used in prayer are naturally ancient: it is hardly possible to pinpoint their origin.

In all ages people have prayed on bended knee, where kneeling is in fact a reduced, stylized form of throwing oneself to the ground. The ancient world, in its unvarnished harshness, called this touching-of-the-forehead-to-the-floor *proskynesis* (Greek: "lying down like a dog"), the dog's gesture of humility, pressing its head to the ground before its master as a sign of subjection. This action seems, for all genuine religious feeling, to be the most natural. In Islam it accompanies public prayer, among the Orthodox it accompanies the veneration of icons, reliquaries, and the offertory gifts during the liturgy; and, among the Catholics, new priests lie with their face to the floor during their consecration. One of the prime examples of this style of prayer is Moses, who threw himself before the burning bush, and what else could he have sensibly done at that moment? The advantage of this style of obeisance is that, in so doing, once does not actually have to say—perhaps even think—anything. The gesture speaks for itself. All the more pity that, for around the last two hundred years in the West, it no longer appears to be socially acceptable. The forms of temporal power have changed, but that does not mean that God has to be satisfied with the marks of respect due to a Federal President. As alarming as complete and absolute dominion over earth may seem to be, God is not a constitutional monarch; even those who do not believe in Him know that.

A lesser form of the *proskynesis* is the bow, much practiced by the Jews and Muslims at prayer—one thinks of those praying before the Wailing Wall, making an almost infinite number of small bows one after the other. Yet a correctly prayed "Gloria" during the Catholic Mass looks almost exactly the same. The "Glory be to the Father and to the Son and to the Holy Spirit" is said bowed by Catholics and Orthodox; at that point, the name of Jesus is also honored with a bow of the head.

Just as old as the prostration in prayer is the stretching-of-oneself-into-the-heights; one could name this form of prayer —standing, with outstretched arms and face turned to heaven—"the prayer of Ganymede" (in Goethe's sense: a lifting of oneself to meet the divinity who comes down from heaven in the form of an eagle). Practiced by pharaohs and Greek pagans, it was also adopted by the early Christians. Archaeologists call it the attitude of the *orante* (Latin: "praying") found in frescoes of the catacombs. In the Orthodox Church the priest prays in this way when he looks upon the image of the Pantokrator in the vault of the apse.

It is utterly clear to the person who prays that God is above. Theologically he may know that God is bound to no particular locale, that there is no "above" and "below" in the universe. Yet praying Christians will feel themselves supported in their almost physical conviction that God is "above" by the practice of Jesus, who lifted His eyes to heaven in prayer, for instance at the Last Supper. It is remarkable and instructive to note that those who pray as believers of the "religions of the Book" never adopt attitudes of prayer that are in any way relaxed, therapeutic, and comfortable. To relax in prayer is not a Western concept. The Lotus position and sitting cross-legged—

practices that accompany far-Eastern mediation—are not initially easy to adopt, but they make it possible for the experienced practitioner to persevere through many hours of self-absorption; yet they are—for good reasons—not attitudes of prayer that ought be adopted by Christians, Jews, and Muslims. The prayer of the latter is directed at a being who is substantially and fundamentally separate from them. The one who is prayed to is not the same as the one who prays. That is only taken as a matter of course from the perspective of the religions of the Book—not, by the way, any longer taken for granted in Christianity, since syncretic, psychologizing, and secularizing tendencies have drawn man and God almost inseparably together. However, the classic Christian at prayer speaks with God as with another person, completely independent of him and his own conceptions. This person stands above him. The person praying, aware of his own imperfections, tries either to enlarge this chasm yet further, or diminish it in exalted love. In the religions of the Book the attitudes of prayer express the idea that God is not in the same place as the one praying to Him. In Latin, one of the verbs for the act of worship is *adorare*, whose root, if traced back to its most ancient origins, is related to the Latin word *os*, the mouth, as in *osculum*, the kiss. In the Italian south the faithful cross themselves upon entering a church or upon glimpsing a Marian image and then kiss their index finger. As in ancient times, they greet the divinities with an implicit blown kiss. Those who pray resemble people standing upon the quay and sending kisses to their relatives who lean against the rail of the departing ship.

    That God is not where we are is most clearly expressed in the prayerful practice of processions and pilgrimages. The psalm *Judica* (Latin: "Judge me, O God") that stands at the beginning of the traditional Catholic Mass describes the spiritual movement which is expressed in the wandering of a prayerful man to a sacred site. In this psalm the distance of God is experienced as the absence of God, which unleashes sorrow and confusion. The *discernatio* (discernment or distinction) leads out of this agonizing state: separation from the *gens non sancta*, the unholy people—to which the one praying admittedly himself belongs, but which he now wishes to leave. Perhaps this separation is only a line drawn in the dust of the earth, the boundary between those who are holy and those who are unholy, which the prayerful man now consciously crosses in order to reach the "holy mountain and the holy tent." The sacred is not within the one who prays, but beyond him. He does not seek himself in prayer, but rather something else; and if that prayer is the desire to depart from oneself and one's own unholiness, it longs for unmistakable signs showing that one has left behind one's own will. Subjection to prescribed acts and forms is accompanied by the hope that, in the separation of holy from unholy people, the first step may possibly already have been taken.

The Repetitions of the Angel

The rosary, that prayer chain of individual beads which are moved by the one at prayer, probably originally comes from India and is there, in any case, in constant use by the meditating monks and sadhus. The Muslims immerse themselves, with the help of their "rosary," in the hundred names of God; the Orthodox use it for the practice of the "heart prayer"; and the Catholics have connected it with an order of prayer that is intended to help them to view in prayer all the stages of salvation history connected with Jesus. The Feast of the Rosary is celebrated on the day of the Christian victory over the Turkish fleet at Lepanto, because the Christians attributed their success to the intercession of the Mother of God; this confirmation of a technique of prayer which is also familiar to Islam proves, once more, that war often brings hostile cultures closer together. Even the Angelus bells are suggested by the call of the Islamic Muezzin from the minaret.

Like the Eastern prototypes, the rosary is also based upon

the foundation of repetition, though these repetitions are structured almost architectonically and logically; their number is not a matter for the person praying, as accords with the somewhat rationalistic nature of the Latin language. The closed chain contains an appendage: a cross and five beads lead up to the circlet of prayer. Every celebratory prayer in the whole world begins with the invocation that God may assist the prayer and even make it possible. Those who pray are conscious of the fact that they are unreliable and distracted in prayer and do so with questionable motives, and that they are dependent even in prayer upon divine assistance. What Paul assures us, namely that the Holy Spirit completes every incomplete prayer with His power and that, given this assurance, there cannot be any such thing as an incomplete prayer: this, though the individual may occasionally feel little disposed to pray, appears to be similarly felt across the globe. The one who prays signs himself with the sign of the cross at the sentence *Adjutorium nostrum in nomine Domini qui fecit caelum et terram* ("Our help is in the name of the Lord who made heaven and earth") and thereby places himself under the cross. It belongs among the particularities of Christianity that prayer and sacrifice, the *opus Dei,* can be similarly understood—as is possible in the Latin—as "work for God" and the "work of God" Himself. Thereby Catholic doctrine intentionally leaves unclear the extent to which the prayer is to be attributed to the one who prays and the measure in which it is to be attributed to divine assistance. Subjectively speaking, the step from the profane realm into the sacred, which stands at the beginning of every prayer, remains a risk, something ventured. "May the act succeed!" announces the ringmaster of the Chinese circus before each new number. Similarly, he who prays must sense that he is held in indissoluble tension between trust in divine assistance and mistrust of his own person, on whose turning to God in prayer everything appears to depend (but perhaps it doesn't, either!).

 The rosary consists, after the introductory prayers, of five blocks of ten "*Ave Maria*s," which are separated from one another by a "*Pater noster.*" The principle of repetition, upon which every ancient prayer rests, is here connected with the essential requirement of specific "content," instruction, theological reflection; for every block of "Ave Marias" stands under the sign of an incident from the New Testament: in the "Joyful Mysteries" it is the childhood of Jesus that is examined, in the "Sorrowful Mysteries" the Passion, and in the "Glorious Mysteries" the resurrection and the advent of the Kingdom of God. Nonetheless, the most important thing about this prayer remains the repetition, even if the change in the image to be reflected on somewhat weakens it. The repetition creates a sense of timelessness and this feeling mediates an anticipation of eternity, which is indeed timelessness. Repetition facilitates the experience of moving forwards while remaining, in time, stationary. In the churches of the south the rosary is to be found at its most meaningful. Two choirs, each comprised of a pair of old ladies seated in the left and right banks of pews respectively, alternate the prayer: one group says the first half of the "Ave Maria" in a higher register, the other answers with the second half in a lower register. The prayer is rattled off mechanically. Those who pray conduct themselves almost like seamstresses at an old sewing machine, driving a powerful propeller that, after a while, gently and effortlessly raises them into the air.

In religious doctrine repetition originates, as a fundamental of prayer, in the practice of the angels and archangels. The visions of the Old Testament show the angels at their sole activity, which is also the sole purpose of their existence: the praise of God. "*Sanctus, sanctus, sanctus,*" call the two seraphim, one to another in uninterrupted repetition. The prayer of the angels accords with the Pauline admonition to Christians "to pray unceasingly." The monks of the Greek and Russian Orthodox take this demand seriously and attempt to truly adhere to it in imitation of the angels. "Without ceasing"— that means even during work and eating, during recreation and possibly even during sleep. There is not room enough here to portray the Orthodox technique of the "prayer of the heart" in the necessary detail. Still, the "prayer of the heart" has nothing to do with an edifyingly lyrical name; rather, it is the utterly factual description of a program with the goal—after essential practice—of connecting one's heartbeat indissolubly to prayer. One sentence—"Jesus Christ, Son of God, have mercy on me"—is initially repeated fifty or one hundred times, then ever more often, until it is associated with breathing in and out, and becomes one with the rhythm of the heart. In the beginning, with this practice, one uses the Orthodox rosary of a ring made of knots, without the spaces of the Latin rosary; but there eventually comes a time when such tactile aides are superfluous. It is worth noting that the teachers of the prayer of the heart do not demand any sort of compulsory concentration from their students. They are advocates of the "praying with the lips" which in our world is seen as mere pretense. In the affirmation of corporeality that characterizes all authentic ascetics, they mistrust intellectual concepts and value the action of the body at least as highly as acts of the mind. The body that rests upon its knees and moves its lips in prayer is superior to the diffuse, distracted, doubting and quarrelsome mind and, in the long run, will conquer it. Those who diligently apply themselves to the prayer of the heart find that, gradually and then increasingly, it takes over ever greater portions of the day. It ultimately becomes independent of the will: those who know the prayer of the heart speak of being woken by prayer during the night or in the morning—this prayer continues through sleep. The result is that he who prays acquires a constantly increasing distance from all that surrounds him, but particularly from ambition, possessions, the craving for recognition and even from the concern for his own person. The ego having placed itself under an alien yoke, now discovers that what awaited it there was freedom.

Christmas Every Day

To have to celebrate Christmas every day is probably a rather strange idea, even for enthusiasts of that particular celebration. Yet it did not always possess the unique individuality that has accrued to its celebration, particularly in recent centuries. In the early decades of Christianity, particularly in those communities formed by Paul, there was no Christmas and there were not supposed to be any feasts at all. What Jesus had done was, in the eyes of those early Christians, so great that no further progression of history seemed possible. The baptized lived in expectation of the return of Jesus and no longer wished to have anything to do with a routine associated with a calendar. The new life existed in a timelessness in which all of salvation history came nearer to the ahistorical present. The celebration of feasts and thereby the return to *time* occurred, for Christians, at the same time as there arose the need to rediscover the locations of that salvation history. The feasts were, in a temporal form, what Jerusalem or Bethlehem signified for the pilgrim: stations by means of which the long awaited return became a movement, a step toward destiny.

As it came to the issue of naming a date for the "Feast of the Nativity of Our Lord according to the Flesh," as Christmas is called amongst the Orthodox, no one was concerned to find out the precise, correct, "civilly recorded" birthday of Jesus. Apparently none of the disciples or evangelists were interested in it. The attempts, by means of certain stellar conjunctions which are supposed to correspond with the Star of Bethlehem, to ascertain the date with astronomical certainty is characteristic of the modern age. There is no doubt that the 25th of December—which was finally proclaimed to be Christmas in the fourth century after Christ—was exclusively chosen with the

Subversive Catholicism

eyes of faith. There has long been conjecture that the Christians had wanted to institute the feast of the nativity of Jesus on a date which replaced a pagan feast, such as that of the late Roman "Sol invictus" perhaps, or a German solstice festival, and Christian rhetoric—with its comparisons between Christ and the sun—seemed to corroborate this conjecture. The truth is otherwise. It was not even the date of the 25th of December, with its pagan festival, which engaged the Church Fathers' attention: they looked to a completely different date, the 25th of March which, according to ancient Jewish tradition, was the day on which God began the work of creation. By taking this date as the day on which Mary received the angel's annunciation of her son, conceived by the Holy Spirit, the 25th of December—nine months later—gave the date of the nativity as a matter of course.

In the eyes of the Church Fathers the genesis of the world and the mysterious hour of Nazareth, in which an angel entered into the house of a young girl, possessed the same weight: both events were the immaculately symmetrical counterpart of the other, alien enough for our age which experiences rationality and faith as opposites. Just as God created the world out of nothing—a world that then drifted away from Him—so he also created the body of His Son out of nothing, without the cooperation of man, in the body of a virgin in order to bring the same world back to Him; a sort of redemptive switch as in the chess move ("castling"), in which God became man in order that man might become God. The counterpart to the beginning of Genesis—"In the beginning God created the heavens and the earth"—is the famous prologue to the Gospel of John—"In the beginning was the Word"—which defines what occurred at the birth of Jesus: "and the Word became flesh."

Becoming flesh, incarnation, is the new concept which this Gospel pericope brought into the world. This concept contains the core of Christian faith, which does not essentially differentiate itself from other religions in its view of the creation of the world or in cultural or moral teaching, but rather in the conviction that the Creator God took on the form of his own creation, in order to allow man to return to his old, lost image of God. "And the Word became flesh and dwelt among us": until recently, Catholics only said or heard this concluding sentence on their knees. Even the priest who proclaims the Gospel of Christmas morning bends the knee at this sentence. It was the *arcanum* (Latin, "the secret") of the Christian religion; it was on this point that those who only wished to venerate Jesus of Nazareth as a great, God-filled man were differentiated from Christians. It took one thousand years for the beginning of the Gospel according to John—the proclamation of the creation of the world / Christmas—to emerge from the Christmas Mass and enter into every Catholic Mass. In the thirteenth century Thomas Aquinas placed the doctrine which originates in apostolic times—that Jesus is truly present in the forms of bread and wine at the Eucharistic sacrifice—upon the basis of Aristotelian philosophy. He developed the new terminology with which both the true presence of the Redeemer and the consecration of the sacrificial offerings into His flesh and blood was to be conceptualized: that of "real presence" and "transubstantiation." The crowning glory of this philosophical penetration was the Feast of Corpus Christi, in which the presence of Christ in the form of bread was to be particularly venerated. Thomas compiled texts for the new Mass of Corpus Christi and composed a long didactic poem, the sequence "Lauda Sion," which became so popular for this particular liturgy that it even earned its own satirical send-up in the "Carmina Burana."

For the "preface" of the Mass of Corpus Christi, the philosopher—never lost for words—harked back to an already existing prayer: the "preface" of Christmas. This connection between the Eucharistic sacrifice and Christmas is still today sometimes understood as a stopgap solution. But the wording of the prayer makes instantly clear what Thomas had in mind: "that visibly knowing God, we may be drawn by Him to the love of things invisible"—which could relate equally to the child in the crib as much as to the Host which is elevated above the priest's head during the consecration. This offering of the consecrated gifts of bread and wine is intended to allow the crucifixion to become tangible. Thomas, in his systematic manner of thought, knew that, if the Eucharistic Christ is to be killed (sacrificed), he must first have been alive. What occurred at the consecration was thus not only sacrifice and death, but also birth: Christ was born on the altar in order subsequently to be sacrificed there. The cloths which bedecked the altar not only represented the shroud of Jerusalem, but also the swaddling cloths of Bethlehem. At the time Corpus Christi was founded, the Christmas Gospel—"In the beginning was the Word"—was first placed in the Dominican Missal and thereafter into every Missal as the final gospel of each and every Mass. The priest read it after the final blessing in a quiet voice and knelt, as at Christmas, for the final phrase, whether reading it aloud or singing it. "In the beginning was the Word" became the résumé of the liturgy, the sum of all its many words and actions. "We have seen His glory—that of the incarnate Word": that was meant to be said of every Mass in which one had glimpsed the solemnly displayed Host.

Why was this Christmas final gospel removed from the Mass? Perhaps because people had forgotten what it was supposed to express? The misremembering or ignorance of the significance of liturgical details is actually no great loss for the liturgy itself and its meaningful execution. The best elements of a symphony can also be conveyed to those who have no understanding of counterpoint or the circle of fifths. Nonetheless, one must know that there is no element in the liturgy—no matter how small—that does not conceal behind it something of consequence. Thus the final gospel, which first crept into the liturgy in the Middle Ages, proves how faithful the Church, in her Mass, had remained to the ideal of the Apostles: to celebrate Good Friday and Easter every day, as well as Christmas.

By Their Fruits You Shall Know Them...

Six Theses on the Liturgical Reform

Thesis 1: *The break with tradition*

THE REFORM of the Mass undertaken by Paul VI in the wake of the Second Vatican Council is a unique event in the Church's history. Never before had the Church forbidden an ancient rite; never before had the Church substituted a "manufactured" rite (in the words of Cardinal Ratzinger) for one that had grown organically over the centuries. The rite that characterized the Western Church until 1968 is by no means "Tridentine" if by that we mean "created by" the Council of Trent (1545–1563)—as people often imagine erroneously—but goes back, in its Western elements, to Gregory the Great (590–604). It was the rite of the pope and of the city of Rome, made binding on the universal Church when, after the Reformation, heretical elements had infiltrated many local rites.

The Council of Trent, however, did conduct an intensive debate regarding this traditional rite. It acknowledged that it contained no unimportant or subordinate parts; everything in it fitted together perfectly and in detail. The liturgy was a living organism: it was impossible simply to remove parts of it—like removing a stone from a building and replacing it with something else—without damaging the whole. This organism was nothing other than an icon of the Incarnation. Like all other ancient religions, the purpose of the Christian cult (or "worship") was to render the Divine present. The old Mass was concerned with making the God-Man present: in this sacrament

Subversive Catholicism

God once again took flesh, and once again was born, died, and rose from the dead. In the most ancient theology, which is still a living reality in the Orthodox Church, what was made present in the Mass was not the Last Supper but, above all, the Lord's sacrificial death on the Cross.

Shortly before it withered and faded away, the worldview that we call "secularization" (in its various forms) penetrated the Church. It regarded concepts such as sin, guilt, sacrifice and redemption as the dregs of an ancient, barbarous, and long-forgotten religion that was now an embarrassment to our "advanced" human race. Accordingly this traditional sacrament had to be reinterpreted as a peace-bringing memorial meal celebrated by the community. Since then the Church has been dominated by an insoluble contradiction: the pope's teaching has not ceased to proclaim the traditionally binding teaching on the Eucharistic sacrament, whereas the practice of the faith (which, in religion, is always much more important than the doctrine) has more or less abandoned this traditional view; in many lands it has already implanted a totally new mentality among the faithful. If the papal teaching office (*magisterium*) continues to fail in its duty to incarnate its teaching in the practice of the universal Church, the destructive consequences of this contradiction will not be long in coming.

Thesis 2: *The new Mass is not the Mass of Vatican II*

The postconciliar liturgical reform cannot draw its legitimacy from the Constitution on the Liturgy *Sacrosanctum Concilium* of the Second Vatican Council. What the council fathers had in mind in this Constitution is absolutely clear. Above all, they demanded extreme caution in the examination of the liturgical books. They forbade all change in the liturgy except what would promise "definite advantage." They confirmed the binding nature of Latin as the language of worship, making exceptions for the vernacular only for pastoral reasons. Here they were thinking of the mission territories outside Europe—and it was precisely in such lands that there was no particular difficulty about a "cultic" language. The council fathers desired that the readings and gospels should be read in the vernacular, and that the psalm *Judica* be dropped, together with the Prologue of St. John at the end of Mass. They desired that there be no further "unnecessary repetitions." Chiefly, this latter requirement meant that the priest should not (for instance) say the Gloria and Credo quietly by himself while the people said or sang them aloud: he should utter these prayers together with the community.

Under Paul VI, the missal was modified in accord with these ideas; a missal was published in 1965 that reflected the wishes of the council fathers. Deviations from the latter were minimal; the actual form of worship was not affected. What we know as today's Mass—or rather, *Masses,* since no obligatory type exists any more—would have had no chance of being accepted by the council fathers. The shift from the sacrificial celebration, oriented to God, to what we generally find today, namely, a community-orientated meal-celebration, was not what the council fathers wished. The most important elements of the Mass as practiced today—where the priest faces the people (and not, as formerly, where priest and people prayed together facing east), and communion in the hand, not in the mouth—are not even to be found in the Mass reform of Paul VI. They were practices extorted from Rome in a spirit of disobedience to the prescriptions of the missal. The paradoxical result is that a Mass celebrated according to the old missals is considerably closer to the council fathers' intentions than a Mass according to the *Novus Ordo,* even in the rare cases where the latter is celebrated with appropriate dignity and according to what the missal lays down.

Thesis 3: *The aim of the reform was not to strengthen discipline, but to weaken it*

In the past, the aim of every reform in the Church had been the re-establishing of discipline, the revitalizing of some Church order that had fallen into decay. When we speak of the *Ecclesia semper reformanda* we are referring to the human fact that there is a tendency to throw off burdens and blunt the imposed rules. The monastic reforms of Cluny and Citeaux, and of the Carmelites, and the reforms introduced by the Council of Trent, are associated with a return to a stricter order, a tightening of the reins, a return to a more radical religious practice and a restoration of a spiritual discipline that had been lost.

The postconciliar liturgical reform is the first reform in the history of the Church that did not have the aim of re-establishing order, but of softening, abolishing, and relativizing it. Nowadays every liturgical order is *de facto* optional. Confession has been largely abolished. The duty of fasting has been reduced to two days in the year, and as for the Eucharistic fast, it has practically disappeared. No longer is there a prescribed liturgical language and liturgical music. Today the exclusive criterion for every kind of liturgy is "can people accept it?" and "is it effective communication?" There is a long list of liturgical practices that can no longer be "imposed" on the modern believer: kneeling is totally impossible, cultic language "does not address people where they are," Mass schedules must be people-friendly, all passages from Holy Scripture that are upsetting or harsh have to be cut out. When the faithful say that "the liturgy does not speak to them," that they "do not feel they have a part in it," and that it "means nothing to them," the theologians' reaction is always to beat a retreat. The parish priest, in dealing with the liturgy committee of his parish council, cannot expect his bishop to back him up. On the contrary, he will be reproached for not having been sufficiently flexible and submissive to parish demands. The liturgical reform has absolutely nothing to do with religious reform in the old meaning of the term. It resembles the frantic "special offer" and "sale" mentality of a supermarket that is fast losing its customers.

Thesis 4: *By its own standards the "pastoral" reform of the Mass has failed*

Pope Paul VI's reform of the Mass puts the emphasis, not on the worship of God, but on the community: on training, catechizing, influencing, and (even) entertaining the community—getting it in the right mood. Here the priest faces the people like a presenter in a TV broadcast: when he says prayers, they are actually—even if he seems to be speaking to God—addressed to the congregation; his aim is to arouse religious feelings in them, he intends to provide spiritual leadership. Just as good teachers try to involve their pupils in the lesson, here the members of the community are to be encouraged to join in the sacred proceedings—otherwise they will get bored. When the priest does something, first of all he likes to explain what he is going to do. On Good Friday, at the hour of Jesus's death, he is to prostrate himself on the floor and, face downwards, utter silent prayer; but he feels it necessary to introduce this action by saying, "Prayer can take many forms; it can consist of words, but also it can be a song or a dance—or even silence." Many priests actually give four or five homilies during the course of the Mass. For the Our Father, the priest calls on everyone to hold hands: these adults stand there just like schoolchildren in their classroom. At the Sign of Peace the priest abandons the altar and goes to shake hands with members of the congregation—which is strange, since they have been together for a considerable time already. The Mass is sometimes punctuated by women and children reading out some passage (perhaps things they have written themselves) while the priest-as-uncle modestly stands to one side and convincingly plays the part of the attentive listener.

The motive behind the reform of the Mass was meant to be

"pastoral." It was meant to stop the faithful hemorrhaging from the Church. The old Mass, of course, was not "pastoral" in this sense: there was no constant squinting at the reaction of the faithful. Mass was often celebrated *in conspectu angelorum*, without anyone else present. In spite of this, although it was not "put on" for the sake of the community, the faithful attended and counted themselves blessed to be able to attend; it uniquely sustained the substance of the faith, the *depositum fidei*. Anyone attending this Mass knew that he was witnessing the presence of Christ. Given the way Mass is celebrated today, such handing-on of the faith cannot be guaranteed. Whole generations of young people have grown up without knowing what a sacrament is, without being able to say the Creed or the Our Father by heart. *This* is the result of a pastorally orientated reform of the Mass. A *pastoral* reform of the Mass has emptied our churches. So we can say that the reform of the Mass, by its own standards, has failed. This unique, astonishing break with the whole religious tradition has failed to keep the faithful in the Church, nor has it succeeded in transmitting the treasure of faith to those remaining in the pews.

Thesis 5: *The reform of the Mass will not stand up to detailed examination*

Contradictory reasons are given for the reform of the Mass; they were trying to kill too many birds with one stone. On the one hand the attempt was made to "modernize" the Church, but this, it was claimed, would correspond to ancient practices. Pius XII (1939–1958) had drawn attention to the danger of "archeologism," i.e., the temptation to impose on the *lex orandi* the results of allegedly "scientific" historical research. Such historical results have the tendency to become antiquated within a few generations; "the latest available knowledge" will be old hat within twenty years. It was thought to be historically certain that in the early Church the Eucharist was celebrated at tables, with the priest facing the congregation. Klaus Gamber's exhaustive research (*The Reform of the Roman Liturgy: Its Problems and Background*) now confirms that, from earliest recorded times, the Church prayed to Christ facing east, toward the rising sun. In the wake of Gamber's examination, what had once been hailed as scientific knowledge is now suspected of being under the influence of ideology.

It was no different with the case of communion in the hand, this proud symbol of the oft-cited "mature Christian." True, in the first centuries communion was received in the hand, but the signs of reverence that accompanied such reception were far greater than that shown in the later usage (i.e., on the tongue, while kneeling): shoes were removed and a cloth was laid over the hands so that they did not come into contact with the transubstantiated Christ. The penitential discipline was harsh. On occasion, sinners had to reckon with several years of exclusion from the sacraments. A member of the Reformed Protestant church once told me that, when he was a youngster, the pastor used to exclude from the Lord's Supper any parishioners who were quarreling with their neighbors; this represents an echo of the actual customs of the first Christian century. Of course the liturgical archeologists did not want to have anything to do with such severity. They were only interested in primitive Christian practices so long as they could be used in a de-sacralizing, profanizing sense.

A particular foe was medieval scholasticism. The scholastic teaching on sacraments was outlawed as obsolete. On the other hand, if it could be used in deconstructing the old Mass, it was occasionally trotted out. The Offertory prayers of the old rite belonged among its most beautiful parts: they included the prayer for the mixing of water and wine ("O God, who, in creating human nature, didst wonderfully dignify it, and hast still more wonderfully restored it...")—a prayer that comes from the fifth century and is the earliest mention of man's dignity, also emphasizing the rite's sacrificial meaning. According to the most ancient liturgical tradition (maintained unbroken in the Eastern Church), the offertory gifts, even prior to being transformed, are handled with the great reverence appropriate to their high destiny. In the desire to reduce the sacrificial character of the Mass, these prayers, which constitute an important link with the Byzantine Rite, had to disappear. At this point the "obsolete" scholasticism was handy enough, in its philosophical and legalistic exactitude, to prove that the Offertory prayers anticipated *inappropriately* the result of transubstantiation, since transubstantiation took place "validly" only after the Lord's words of institution uttered by the priest. The more than fifteen hundred years' reverence for the un-transformed Offertory gifts was wiped away as irrelevant. Its place was taken by a medieval Jewish meal blessing; this underlined the "meal" aspect of the Mass and made no mention of the sacrifice whatsoever.

The ecumenical argument, too, was given weight only when it was a case of de-sacralizing the Mass. The fact that Catholics and Protestants had the same schedule of scriptural readings—in other words, this common feature had survived the break that occurred at the time of the Reformation—was easily jettisoned in order to bring in the new lectionary that was purged of anything that might be thought threatening. None of the novel rules of the new missal would stand up to an examination in the spirit of tradition.

Thesis 6: *The reform of the Mass has produced poisonous fruit*

The reform of the Mass has fostered a profoundly anti-religious attitude among Catholics. Christian worship is no longer a gift of grace that is to be received on one's knees; instead it is a commodity that must be met with mistrust and ill-will, then tested, and often enough rejected. Holy Mass, that formerly was a hermetically closed mystery, had now to open itself up to the confusion of opinions. What previously had been venerated as a super-terrestrial phenomenon is now seen to be something manufactured, something arranged. And what can be arranged, can be rearranged. Now there can be no end of arranging! Anyone can come up with good ideas for changing the liturgy. It is strange, however: the more the Mass is reshaped, the less enthusiasm one has for it. Nowadays parish committees and mass-goers talk about the Mass in the same vein as the aficionados of the state theatre when they discuss a new and only semi-successful staging of a Chekhov play. In Catholic circles, now shrunk to a handful of folk, liturgy has become a banal and paltry thing. In the atmosphere of the new Mass one would never hear—it would be totally unimaginable—a prayer such as this from the Greek Orthodox liturgy (though it perfectly reproduces the spirit of the old Latin liturgy):

> Make us worthy to partake with a pure conscience of Your heavenly and fear-inspiring mysteries from this sacred and spiritual altar, for the remission of sins, for the pardon of transgressions, for the fellowship of the Holy Spirit, for the inheritance of the kingdom of heaven, as a pledge of confidence in You, and not for judgment or damnation.

"Fear-inspiring"—this would hardly get past a contemporary liturgy committee. Nowadays one does not expect to go with head bowed to meet one's Maker and Redeemer, but rather one relaxes in an armchair, waiting for him to arrive. If God has become man, let him take a language course so that he can make himself understood among human beings. It is instructive to observe a "reform" Christian who happens to have found himself at one of the rare celebrations of the old Mass. He stretches out his hands at communion-time, trying to insist that the holy communion be placed in his hand and not on his tongue. He insists on his "right" and waits to see whether the priest will dare to refuse him. If this is the result of the reform of the Mass, one can only say:

"By their fruits you shall know them."

The Old Roman Missal: Between Loss and Rediscovery

THE HISTORY of the Holy Catholic Church is full of mysteries, good and evil; the apostle Paul did not talk for nothing of the "mysterium iniquitatis" as he pulled the rug from under the feet of the question of theodicy—perennial and, over the centuries, ever raised anew—by acknowledging (though radically refusing to answer) that question which arises from a deep-seated sense of unease: Why? Why is there evil amidst God's creation? I am not going to say whether the mystery I am speaking about is good or bad or an indissoluble combination of the two elements; it is true of every great historic event in history that its consequences send their ripples through the centuries and assume ever new appearances. What is a malediction in one century may turn out to be a blessing for a future time; illnesses, on the other hand, can perpetuate themselves with new symptoms.

I write this preamble full of trepidation: I do not approach this subject frivolously. I am talking about the violent upheavals in the history of the Church after the Second Vatican Council; something completely new occurred then, something which had until then never been thought possible. When a Catholic hears the concept "new" used in relation to the Church, he should always be alarmed. The sole new and novel event of world history—the incarnation of God—has already occurred; it does not cease to appear new—it is the "new" which is never completely to be grasped, which points to and anticipates the re-creation of the world after the end of time. However, until that time it sticks in the world's flesh, a thorn of discontent and vexation.

Subversive Catholicism

Next to Jesus Christ, nothing can be new if it is not completely permeated by Him. On the contrary: anything that seeks to modify, to surpass, to re-color, to overtrump the once-for-all revelation—to bring about something "new" in relation to revelation (interesting as it may be, brilliant as it may sound)—will necessarily always be questionable and possibly even dangerous. There is a cultural axiom: the old is good. This accords with the experience of practically every culture. Culture is inevitably connected to confidence in the tradition: culture consists in the enlargement of a human life, in its brevity, into the breadth of the past and the future. Culture enables a man to make the experiences of earlier generations his own and extend them to future generations; to plant trees on the ground of the experience of past generations, the fruit of which will only be enjoyed by coming generations. What is old has shown itself to have the power to persist over many generations. It has not expired like that which is worthless, like dead matter, but rather has proved fruitful over the centuries or perhaps even millennia. On this point Goethe, the great poet of the Germans, remarked: "Only what is fruitful is true." So what is old and has yet remained vital can be—can become—the visible form of truth.

Christians have a further reason to hold fast to the old, to what has been handed down. Their belief in the divinity of Jesus Christ is not comparable to belief in the myths of the pagans, which live in an ahistorical realm of the eternal present. Christians believe that the creator of the heavens and the earth, at a very particular moment in history—in the early days of Imperial Rome—in the most despised province of the Roman Empire, became man. In one of their most sacred texts, the Creed—alongside the name of the Son of God and his Holy Mother—they place the name of a mediocre, ineffective provincial Roman bureaucrat called Pontius Pilatus, the man who, through his weakness, became a participant in the work of salvation and who owes his immortal remembrance solely to the will of the fathers of the Council of Nicea; men who made the historicity of Jesus a constituent element of Christian faith. God became man, and this implied a particular country, a particular language, particular traditions; it meant being born in a particular political and social situation. Jesus was a Jew and at the same time a Roman subject. As His Church thus adopted Jewish and Roman attributes and combined them within herself, she continued—quite literally—the incarnation of God that she is to portray until the end of time. Thus all Christians remain faced toward the future, to the return of the Lord. Yet in order to know *who* is to return they must look back, into the past; but not back into the infinite blackness of the earliest beginnings, but rather to the decades of Augustus and Tiberius. To that time in which the witnesses to His glory lived, those who went to their deaths for their faith—which was actually rather more knowledge than faith—and who have passed the faith on to us. A Christian priest or lay person who stands up for Christianity can never have anything more or better to say, in his own justification, than what Paul formulated: "I have handed on what I received."

Christians, according to the definition of their faith, stand in a chain that binds the present with the past: through the physical act of laying on hands, which cannot be replaced by any spiritualism, they are bound to the apostles of the earliest hours. From them we have learnt that the presence of Christ is the life of His Church, though not in the form of an act of auto-suggestion, of meditation, of internal disposition, but rather in the transformed figure of the incarnate Christ passing before us; Christ, who blesses by laying on his hands, from whose clothes miraculous powers emanate, whose feet were washed by the woman who was a sinner and pierced by the nails, who wept over Lazarus and fried a fish for his disciples. Jesus had taught the apostles that they should continually establish his presence anew; his presence, which was infinitely more precious than his teaching because it contained the whole of those teachings—as well infinitely more besides, accessible only to sight and not to comprehension. In short, the apostles ought to be his instruments, making him present. And this making-present was to be the realization of the highest and most concentrated moment of his earthly life: the moment of His sacrificial death on the cross. Thus the Christians of early times naturally understood that the worship which the Lord had left behind Him was far more than the repetition of the Last Supper; that this meal itself was but a sign of the actual redemptive work which was consummated in death by torture upon the cross.

For that reason they clothed this worship in the most beautiful and sublime forms that mankind had developed for its services of prayer and sacrifice in the millennia before the arrival of the Redeemer; forms which had no author, which were not founded by wise men, but which rather grew from the sentiment of all men who wished to venerate the divinity. Only one thing differentiated this new Christian sacrificial service from its predecessors in all religions: since it made present the sacrifice of Jesus, it was now no longer the work of pious men, but rather the work of God Himself. It was a work that God performed for men; a work which men—even the most pious—could never have performed themselves, but which they were allowed to approach only through the mercy of the Savior. This is a central notion for Christian worship, without which it would be completely incomprehensible: it is not a work of man, nor should it appear to be a work of man. In its form it must show clearly that it does not owe its origins to the wishes of men, but rather to the will of God. These ought to be matters of course for every Catholic, yet we have to admit that in many parts of the Catholic world—particularly in the historic heartlands of the Catholic Church—it is not so.

After this long preamble I now turn back to developments after the Second Vatican Council, in which it was precisely this unheard-of "new something" that appeared—something that Catholics can observe only with dismay. I have attempted to describe the relationship of the Church to her liturgy: it was for almost two thousand years the undisputed corporeal presence

The Old Missal: Between Loss & Rediscovery

of Christ, the Head of the Church—it was in this way that the liturgy was the visible body of the Church. This visibility is no small thing for a Catholic; it is not subordinated to some higher, invisible world, since the time God Himself took on human form and even bore His wounds with him into the state of transfiguration. Ever since the God-Man saw with our eyes and heard with our ears, our senses—which by their very construction are so exposed to deception—are essentially capable of perceiving the truth: through the Incarnation of Christ the material of the world is no longer a realm of deception; rather, since then, matter has once again become recognizable as God's thought in material form.

This is the origin of the absolute seriousness with which the Church treated all physical acts of the liturgy: every hand movement, every bow, every genuflection, every kiss of the consecrated objects, the candles, the vessels, finally the sacrificial offerings of bread and wine, but also even the language in which the divine thoughts expressed themselves—all these were seen in a literal sense as revelation. The Church Father of the East, St Basil the Great, thus expressly referred to the Holy Mass as revelation, just like the Holy Scriptures. A small example sheds light upon the attitude of the pre-Vatican II Church to the material world embraced in her sacraments: the Cistercians of the Middle Ages often engraved the name of Mary on the golden chalice used in the Mass; just as Mary's body had borne the God-Man, so the chalice contains the divine blood. In this way the entire recounting of salvation history flowed into the objects that were used in the Eucharist. The Second Vatican Council had once again comprehensively and expressly confirmed the theology of the Mass that had been handed down; it solemnly recognized sacral language, sacred music—Gregorian Chant, which floats between Occident and Orient and belongs to no single sphere of culture—and only encouraged a cautious review of the liturgical books, as was common practice once every few hundred years, in order to clear out misunderstandings which had crept in.

Subversive Catholicism

Let us once more consider what the Catholic liturgy had already achieved up until this point. Originating in Asia Minor, it had conquered the Greek and Roman world. It finally triumphed in the pagan Imperium, yet had survived the latter's downfall and won the pagan peoples of the north for itself. It became the instrument of a missionary success that was without parallel in the history of the world. It survived so many ruptures in history, so many cataclysms! It exceeded the boundaries of Europe and came to Asia, Africa, and America—everywhere it was at first something alien, for the Germans and the Irish as much as for the Indians, Singhalese, and Chinese. The Germans could neither understand Latin nor even read when the great missionary Boniface brought them the Holy Mass; and it remained so for a long time, principally in the most resplendent epochs of the Church, in which the faithful felt that in the celebration of the Holy Mass it was not primarily about understanding each of its words, but rather experiencing the presence of the Redeemer; that he who understood every single word of the Mass but did not experience this presence had—strictly speaking—not understood a thing about it. Revolutions broke out across the world, dictatorships arose and fell, but the Holy Mass remained ever the same. For the whole world the Holy Mass was the comprehensible expression of the immutability of the Church throughout time. Even the enemies of the Church recognized that her strength lay in her timelessness; not in the sense of being outdated, but because her liturgy was not completely identified with any one epoch, any one culture: it always stood one step removed from time, and so it stood in every epoch. It was not celebrated in the present but rather "per omnia saecula saeculorum"—for all times since the creation of the world, until the apocalypse, and then in eternity, which had already begun. It is this eternity that stands as the gold-leaf backdrop behind every historical age and which is celebrated forever in this liturgy—the "marriage of the lamb" as the Book of Revelation calls it.

I must again pick up the thread which I keep letting fall; I do

The Old Missal: Between Loss & Rediscovery

this, as I now realize, out of a certain reluctance to recount what actually happened. I can conceive of plenty of sociological, political, and historical reasons for this unique incident in history which, as a trenchant event with far-reaching consequences, is perhaps only to be compared to the century of iconoclasm in Constantinople, though the effect of the iconoclasm only encompassed a small region when compared with the wide regions of the global Catholic Church. Yet these reasons do not convince me: I am not satisfied with the chronicle of vanity, of blindness and naivety which accompanied the drastic surgery of Pope Paul VI and his advisors. I believe in the supernatural nature of the Church and therefore natural explanations as to her triumphs and her catastrophes do not satisfy me. So I refrain from guessing or supposing which precise reasons it was that brought Pope Paul and many of the bishops of his time to abandon the inherited treasure, the heart of the Church, and to design a new liturgy which—as Pope Benedict has said—may well have been formed from elements of the old liturgy, but with a slant that was in many ways opposed to that old liturgy. The reform—which, I must reiterate, was a deep surgical attack, unlike anything in the history of the Churches, and which was therefore something fundamentally new—was particularly ill-starred, not only as regards the intentions of the reformers, but rather as to the point in time at which the reform took place: the year of 1968, still insufficiently interpreted in the study of history.

There are years in which, right across the world—without explicit relation, or intellectual or political connection to one another—there arise related ideas and religious currents; such as the years in which Buddha taught in India, Confucius in China, Zoroaster in Persia, Jeremiah in Israel, and Pythagoras in Greater Greece. Pivot points, these are called: as though all these events turned on one common pivot of the world. In 1968 there broke out across the whole world an insurrection against tradition, against what had been passed down and against authority: in France the last patriarchal head of state

Subversive Catholicism

in the Western world, General de Gaulle, was toppled; in North America there arose a violent youth movement which made it impossible for the government to continue the Vietnam War; in Germany the traditional, highly efficient system of the free universities was struck dead; in Prague there emerged a rebellion against the Soviet Union; and in China there reigned the great Cultural Revolution with its immeasurable destruction. In 1969 Pope Paul had promulgated his new Missal—which had come about despite the insistent opinion of a synod of bishops that he himself had convoked—which was the first Missal in the history of the Church to have been compiled and written largely by professors at their desks. And now this reform, which one could just as well call a new creation, fell into the maelstrom of the great year of global revolution. It was precisely in the middle of this completely untamable current of an age, which fundamentally rejected every form of obedience, authority, respect, and reverence, that this radical measure—that was so sharply opposed to the spirit of the Church—was supposed to be enacted across the entirety of the global Church, down to the last Chinese catacomb community. In many places of the world, above all in Western Europe and the United States, it was as if the dams had been breached. What had been untouchable had proved itself touchable—from now on there would no longer be anything untouchable; from now on, everything ought to be able to be organized from scratch by each generation. The reform of Pope Paul went far, but in its realization in the majority of dioceses, in any event in Europe and America, it went much farther and left behind everything which had still bound it to Catholic tradition. Reform, thanks to the pivotal year of 1968, had to become revolution. It began with the liturgy; yet it was now that the central value of the liturgy for the Church was revealed, for indeed everything else—theology, the image of the priest, the hierarchical constitution of the Church, the daily prayers of the faithful, the education of Catholic culture, mission, finally even the core elements of belief—was most intimately connected to the liturgy and stood or fell with it. It was plainly not an optional, historically determined form that could be adapted to the requirements of the day without harm to its content; that must now have been obvious even to those who (mistakenly) thought that love of the traditional liturgy was part of the morally questionable realm of an "aesthetics of the sacred."

Pastoral reasons were given as the most important argument for the reform: a strongly simplified rite, with theologically unassuming prayers that stuck to friendly generalities in the relevant language of the region, this would help to keep the modern man within the Church. This idea should already have caused some scratching of heads, given the fact that in the missionary lands of Asia, with their highly developed cultures, men had for thousands of years been accustomed to extraordinarily rich rites in sophisticated sacral language: to want to deny them the Catholic inheritance seems like an act of colonial paternalism. Yet even in the lands from which Christianity had originated, the simplifying rite had devastating consequences. With its enforced implementation, against some resistance—the last exertion of which Roman centralism was capable—there began the exit of the faithful from the churches. A Catholic aphorist put it thus: "The Mass reforms wished to open the doors of the Church to those who found themselves outside; instead, those who were inside ran out." The solemn and hieratic worship was abolished; the intention was to bring the sacraments to the people, but they shied away from this gift. In wide regions of Europe any understanding of sacraments disappeared; it was a highly puzzling development: now that people could actually understand every word, Eucharistic belief and custom—on the whole—had become alien to the people; the great work of the Church, rendering the Godhead visible, was no longer comprehended. And this went together with the loss of knowledge of Catholic belief. In Europe today there are many Catholics who could barely utter an Our Father or the Creed and who have only the most shadowy conception of the doctrine of the Church.

Subversive Catholicism

The Catholic priesthood sustained a special blow in the period following the reform. In the West the ancient notion that the priest at the altar acts *in persona Christi*—"in the person of Christ"—has faded. The reformed clergy has revamped itself according to a fashionable democratism. It no longer wants to hear of the priest being *homo excitatus a Deo*, "called by God from among men." A modern priest no longer celebrates Mass, he "presides" over it, in the way a party chairman presides over a plenary session. He is oppressed by the idea of differences between laity and priests, which were already evident in the Acts of the Apostles; but he cannot disclaim them and so seeks to make them forgotten. The laity swarm over the sanctuary, women are taking over the altar service; all this makes people forget the fact that acolytes actually belong to the lower strata of clerical ministers. In Europe, the priests have generally laid aside their priestly clothes: they no longer wish to be recognizable, their role has become embarrassing for them in a secularized society. An old saying goes: "A cowl does not make a monk"—and that is correct. But in our own time we have learned that the opposite is equally correct: "Indeed, it is the cowl that makes the monk"—it is primarily the accord between external appearance and spiritual attitude that makes the Catholic priest, who is meant to practice his Christ-role precisely in this physical way, able to be perceived, seen and touched by everyone. *Leiturgia* in Greek means "public service, a service for the public." The priests' prayer stands in contrast to the prayer of the individual, who speaks to God in whatever words come to mind, while the Church prays in the name of the angels, the saints, the souls in purgatory and the living upon the earth and thus, for this reason, this prayer of all for all must be subject to a form that is able to be examined by all. The Church of the West feared that the yawning gap between a libertarian consumer society without religion and the world of faith could open even further, and thus sought to suppress everything which was characteristic of her and which might cause offense in the secular sphere; she forced herself to confirm the modern world in its principles and, as it was said, "to baptize ideas which had not been converted."

Forty years were spent in this way, during which the Church of the West lost ever more of her profile by adapting herself ever more hastily to the views of an areligious society. There is something magical about the numbers: for forty years the people of Israel wandered through the desert, and the Communist occupation of East Germany, with its puppet-regime, also lasted forty years—and when the forty years were up, the fruit ripened, it fell and revealed its foul-smelling contents. One can certainly say that a milieu that is hostile to the Church has hatefully exaggerated, unjustly portrayed, and maliciously generalized the moral scandals with which ecclesial provinces of the West have recently been shaken: but what these scandals show, above all, is the speechlessness and helplessness of a Church that has deliberately secularized herself—in order to make her character, her very nature comprehensible to a public with which she has ceaselessly curried favor. The result of forty years of *aggiornamento*, "bringing up to date," of forty years of popularization and secularization of the sacrament of the altar, is a catastrophe of such grave proportions in the West that it can hardly be exaggerated. As for those who observed the secularization experiment with anxiety and distrust from the very start, they have no sense of triumph or self-righteousness in the face of such a collapse and of the moral ostracism of the Church. We see before us the fact that generations have wantonly been allowed to be lost; the reconstruction will be endlessly hard, will proceed only with enormous effort, and the loss of blood in the Western Church will not be replaced for a long time.

Once before, the Church had to experience a peregrination of faith, leaving its acquired lands and conquering new territory. In the original lands of Christianity—in Palestine, Egypt, Asia Minor, primarily in those places where the young Church blossomed and the first significant councils took place—very few Christians now live; why should it be any different with

Christian Europe? The faith wandered across the world from there, and if, in Asia for instance, Christianity still only comprises a minority, it is nonetheless a strong, determined minority which is willing to make sacrifices and which is viewed with respect by the majority. I have come to realize that the damage inflicted on Catholic tradition was less dangerous where it was not bound up with the spirit of 1968. It was certainly possible to enact these reforms, though they clearly infringed Church tradition, with piety and with a heart shaped by the Catholic heritage. Many of the most scandalous contraventions of the law of this Catholic inheritance were not even anchored in the reform of Pope Paul; they arose from the disobedience that spread everywhere in the West following the collapse of order that occurred during the pontificate of this unfortunate pope. Paul VI spoke of this in a moving way as he began to realize the extent of the destruction: "the smoke of Satan has infiltrated the Church." The Missal of Paul VI did not, for example, prescribe the turning-around of the altars—that is the most palpably felt transgression against the tradition of prayer in the whole world. The priest should turn himself, along with the congregation, to the Crucified and to the Christ who will return from the East; he should direct his prayers, in common with the congregation, to the altar and to Christ, present in the form of the offertory gifts: Pope Paul did not necessarily wish to bring these things to an end. This change in the direction of prayer has caused greater harm in Europe and America than all of the relativizing, demythologizing, and humanizing theologies put together. It became patently clear to even the simple faithful that the prayers were directed, not to God, but rather to the congregation, which was to be put in the correct mood so as to celebrate itself as the "people of God." It was similar with the administration of communion in the hand, instead of in the mouth as before. That too was not intended by the Missal of Paul VI, but was exacted by the protestantizing German bishops. Until that point, an entire bouquet of respectful gestures had surrounded the sacrament of the altar, and these gestures were the most effective homily, which continually showed priests and faithful quite clearly the mysterious presence of the Lord under the forms of bread and wine. We can be certain: no theological indoctrination of so-called enlightened theologians has so harmed the belief of Western Catholics in the presence of the Lord in the consecrated Host as the innovation of receiving communion in the hand, accompanied by the abandoning of all care in the handling of the particles of the Host.

Yet can one really not receive communion reverently in the hand? Of course that is possible. Yet once the traditional forms of reverence were in place, exercising their blessed influence on the consciousness of the faithful, their discontinuation contained the message—and not just for the simple faithful—that so much reverence was not really necessary, and along with that there consequently grew the (initially unspoken) conviction that there was *nothing there* that demanded respect.

As we have said, these were the consequences of the unholy combination of the reform of the liturgy with the political *Zeitgeist* of the West, which absurdly promoted a democratization of Catholic worship, as though the Church was a political organization like a state or a party. In Asia, the growth of the Church, her abundance of the Spirit and her charismatic power seem not to have suffered under the reform, and every Catholic must be heartily thankful for that fact. Where the fire burns, it can also be passed on. It would not be the first time in the history of the Church that countries only recently subject to missionary activity themselves give the faith back to the Christian heartland which had lost it. After the fall of the Roman Empire, France was re-Christianized by Irish monks who themselves had Egyptian missionaries to thank for their Christianity: thus the Christian law of reciprocity is fulfilled, in which brothers strengthen one another in their faith. Yet it must also be considered that no man is an island, as the poet John Donne says; even in the global Church there are no "islands of the blessed" that remain permanently untroubled by the fortunes and misfortunes of the whole. The crisis of the large body will one day reach all its parts, and one ought to be prepared for that. And it is also for those regions which have not yet shown symptoms of disintegration and weakness to ask what caused this weakness and how it can be permanently conquered.

The damage inflicted on the inherited liturgy by the reforms of Pope Paul VI remains a problem in the strict philosophical sense of the word; it has created a situation that cannot be solved on the spot. It has been said that "problems do not have a solution, but rather a story." And the story of the problem of liturgical reform has actually only just begun. The Holy Father Pope Benedict XVI, even before his election as pope, belonged among the bishops—unfortunately not too numerous—who knew that the radical break in the tradition of the Church signified a great danger for the Church. In his famous *Motu proprio* [*Summorum Pontificum*] he has now determined that the inherited rite of the Church was never banned, because it was inherently incapable of being banned. The pope is not the master of the liturgy, but rather its guardian. The Church never separates herself from her inherited rites, which she views as spiritual treasure. Rather, she encourages the study of these inherited rites and the unlocking of their hidden value for the present. Concerned to avoid the futile attempt of simply ignoring the past—as though the last forty years had simply not existed—the pope has decided upon an act of determination, primarily with a view to reconciling the party of reform with the defenders of Catholic tradition. According to papal determination there now exists but one Roman Rite which has two forms, the ordinary and the extraordinary, which stand equal to one another, which can be celebrated by every priest at any time without the need for episcopal approval, and which are intended to be related to one another. There is no doubt that the celebrant of the new, the "ordinary" rite, ought to learn from the "extraordinary" inherited rite how ecclesial tradition wishes to understand the Holy Mass. The pope has assigned the Church the task of reacquainting herself with the old books of her rites, in order to

The Old Missal: Between Loss & Rediscovery

learn from the fathers and saints of the past millennia how the solemn work of making God present is to be accomplished.

We are thus all encouraged to open up the old Missal, thankful for having found at the last minute something that was practically lost forever, and discover how the Church (and our forefathers to whom we owe our faith) used to pray. Ultimately we may even attempt to pray in the same way ourselves. One ought not forget that this was the Missal of the Roman popes; it was prescribed for the whole Church by the Council of Trent because it contained, with certainty, not a single error or possibility of misunderstanding. In the great crisis of the Reformation it was almost seen as the spiritual Noah's Ark of the Church, in which she survived amidst the flood of sin resulting from the general loss of faith. We will thus rediscover the psalm *Judica* ("Judge me, O God"), with which the traditional Mass begins at the steps of the altar; this unique attunement to the rite, the demand to depart from one's everyday life, to turn from the world which has forsaken God, to no longer pay attention to the fears and worries and profound doubts, and to go on pilgrimage to the sanctuary of the Lord on the Temple Mount—with this psalm the Holy Mass becomes a pilgrimage, a departure, which leaves behind everything that hampers prayer. Then the priest articulates his confession of sin and the congregation listens to him in silence and prays for the forgiveness of his sins, in order to then confess their own sins to the priest; it is only in this dialogical form that the confession of sin has meaning, for a confession requires a listener who, during the confession, does not himself speak. We again discover the Creed of Constantinople, which was formulated in the struggle against Arianism in order to clarify the Nicene Creed. We too, just like the Church threatened by Arianism, need the confession that Jesus is "God from God, Light from Light, true God from true God": at least in Germany this Credo has almost completely disappeared from the Mass, above all the genuflection at the core statement of our faith, *et incarnatus est de Spiritu Sancto ex Maria virgine et homo factus est*: "He was incarnate by the Holy Spirit of the Virgin Mary, and was made man."[1] We shall read again, with astonishment and amazement, the orations, particularly those on the Sunday after Pentecost, which are verbal works of art—partly by St Jerome himself—and which are also suited for meditation outside the Mass; they lend a unique voice to the Christian relationship between God and man. One of the greatest losses of the Mass reform is the prayers of the Offertory, when the gifts prepared for sacrifice are brought veiled to the altar and the holy event of the sacrifice begins. These prayers originate from the oldest times, yet in them—for the first time in the history of mankind—there is a mention of the dignity of man, which God gave his creatures from the beginning and which was renewed by the sacrificial death of Jesus. The *epiclesis*, the invocation of the Holy Spirit upon the gifts, is also of the greatest significance; the Church of the East attributes to it an essential effect in the act of transformation, but even the Church of the West knows that it is the Holy Spirit that will effect the miracle of the transformation. And then the Roman Canon, which is indeed still contained in the new Missal, but which is prayed in but a few places. In its enumeration of the saints of the city of Rome it binds every sacrifice of the Mass to Rome, to the pope, and therewith the global Church; those who celebrate the Mass enter into it from their homelands and become citizens of Rome, members of the one Church that spans the globe. In a highly significant prayer, this canon binds even this present sacrifice at the altar with the sacrifices of all men of all time: with the sacrifice of Abel, the representative of the original revelation; with the sacrifice of King Melchizedek, who was not a Jew and thus stands for the sacrifice of the non-Jewish peoples; and with the sacrifice of Abraham, in whom the sacrifice upon the cross, this drama between father and son, is anticipated in a clarity that still shocks us. We

---

1. In Germany, it is customary at Mass to recite the Apostles' Creed instead of the Niceno-Constantinopolitan Creed.

are only able to speak in a cursory way here of the richness of form possessed by a ritual language refined over millennia; the old Missal contains a wealth of relationships and interconnections that will also be gradually revealed over decades of celebration. It desires to change the lives of the faithful; it requires lifelong meditation and is not a tool of instant propaganda—rather, one must allow it to slowly permeate the soul. And what of the language of the Missal? The English-speaking faithful will soon be able to use official translations that have eliminated the many misleading simplifications and errors; other peoples, in whom the spirit of modernist defiance is more strongly developed, will have to wait longer. It is all the more important that priests and the faithful, too, acquaint themselves with the mother tongue of the Church, in which her doctrines are preserved in such pregnant brevity and unambiguity. A sacred language has the advantage of not being the language of any one people; one approaches it as one approaches a sacred house: prayer reigns in its rooms, prayer that is stronger than the prayer of the individual, a prayer which is there as by right: all one has to do is associate oneself with it. In this language, the supra-temporal and supra-national Church to which we belong is present. Perhaps the deeper meaning of the current crisis is that we should take this opportunity, instead of sinking into pious routine, to rediscover the visible form of the Church, as one would rejoice to find some precious thing one had believed lost, and to realize—perhaps for the first time—its irreplaceability.

Return to Form: The Fate of the Rite is the Fate of the Church[1]

THE TIMES in which a new form is born are extremely rare in the history of mankind. Great forms are characterized by their ability to outlive the age in which they emerge and to pursue their path through all history's hiatuses and upheavals. The Greek column with its Doric, Ionic, and Corinthian capitals is such a form, as is the Greek tragedy with its invention of dialogue that still lives on in the silliest soap opera. The Greeks regarded tradition itself as a precious object; it was tradition that created legitimacy. Among the Greeks, tradition stood under collective protection. The violation of tradition was called *tyrannis*—tyranny is the act of violence that damages a traditional form that has been handed down.

One form that has effortlessly overleaped the constraints of the ages is the Holy Mass of the Roman Church, the parts of which grew organically over centuries and were finally united after the Council of Trent in the sixteenth century. It was then that the missal of the Roman pope, which since late antiquity had never succumbed to heretical attack, was prescribed for universal use by Catholic Christendom throughout the West. If one considers the course of human history, it is nothing short of remarkable that the Roman Rite has survived the most violent catastrophes unaltered.

Without a doubt, the Roman Rite draws strength and vitality

---

1. Translated from the German by William Carroll and Graham Harrison. This essay appeared in the April 2017 edition of *First Things* and is included here with their kind permission.

from its origin. It can be traced back to the apostolic age. Its form is intimately connected with the decades in which Christianity was established, the moment in history the Gospel calls the "fullness of time." Something new had begun, and this newness, the most decisive turning point in world history, was empowered to take shape, take on form. Indeed, this newness came above all in the assumption of form. God the Creator took on the form of man, his creature. This is the faith of Christianity: In Christ all the fullness of God dwells in bodily form, even in that of a dead body. Spirit takes form. From this point on, this form is inseparable from the Spirit; the Risen One and Savior, returning to his Father, retains for all eternity the wounds of his death by torture. The attributes of corporeality assume infinite significance. The Christian Rite, of which the Roman Rite is an ancient part, thus became an incessant repetition of the Incarnation, and just as there is no limb of the human body that can be removed without harm or detriment, the Council of Trent decreed that, with respect to the liturgy of the Church, none of its parts can be neglected as unimportant or inessential without damage to the whole.

It is said that every apparently new thing has always been with us. Alas, this doesn't seem to be the case. The industrial revolution, science as a replacement for religion, and the phenomenon of the wonderful and limitless increase in money (without a similar increase in its material equivalent) have given rise to a new mentality, one that finds it increasingly difficult to perceive the fusion of spirit and matter, the spiritual content of reality that those who lived in the preindustrial world across thousands of years took for granted. The forces that determine our lives have become invisible. None of them has found an aesthetic representation. In a time that is overloaded with images, they have lost the power to take form, with the result that the powers that govern our lives have an intangible, indeed, a demonic quality. Along with the inability to create images that made even the portrait of an individual a problem for the twentieth century, our contemporaries have

The Fate of the Rite is the Fate of the Church

lost the experience of reality. For reality is always first seized in a heightened form that is pregnant with meaning.

In a period such as the present, unable to respond to images and forms, incessantly misled by a noisy art market, all experimentation that tampers with the Roman Rite as it has developed through the centuries could only be perilous and potentially fatal. In any case, this tampering is unnecessary. For the rite that came from late antique Mediterranean Christianity was not "relevant" in the European Middle Ages, nor in the Baroque era, nor in missionary lands outside Europe. The South American Indians and West Africans must have found it even stranger, if possible, than any twentieth-century European who complained that it was "no longer relevant"—whereas it was precisely among those people that the Roman Rite enjoyed its greatest missionary successes. When the inhabitants of Gaul, England, and Germany became Catholic, they understood no Latin and were illiterate; the question of the correct understanding of the Mass was entirely independent of a capacity to follow its literal expression. The peasant woman who said the rosary during Mass, knowing that she was in the presence of Christ's sacrifice, understood the rite better than our contemporaries who comprehend every word but fail to engage with such knowledge because the present form of the Mass, drastically altered, no longer allows for its full expression.

This sad diminution of spiritual understanding is to be expected, given the atmosphere in which the revision of the Roman Rite was undertaken. It was done during the fateful years around 1968, the years of the Chinese Cultural Revolution and a worldwide revolt against tradition and authority after the conclusion of the Second Vatican Council. The council had upheld the Roman Rite for the most part and emphasized the role of Latin as the traditional language of worship, as well as the role of Gregorian chant. But then, by order of Paul VI, liturgical experts in their ivory towers created a new missal that was not warranted by the provisions for renewal set forth by the council fathers. This overreaching caused a breach in the dike. In a short time, the Roman Rite was changed beyond recognition. This was a break with tradition like nothing the Church in its long history has experienced—if one disregards the Protestant revolution, erroneously named "the Reformation," with which the post-conciliar form of the liturgy actually has a great deal in common.

The break would have been irreparable had not a certain bishop, who had participated in the council (and signed the Constitution on the Sacred Liturgy in good faith, assuming that it would be the standard for a "careful" review of the sacred books) pronounced an intransigent "no" to this work of reform. It was the French missionary archbishop Marcel Lefebvre and his priestly society under the patronage of Saint Pius X whom we have to thank that the thread of tradition, which had become perilously thin, did not break altogether. This marked one of the spectacular ironies in which the history of the Church is rich: the sacrament, which has as its object the obedience of Jesus to the will of the Father, was saved by disobedience to an order of the pope. Even someone who finds Lefebvre's disobedience unforgiveable must concede that, without it, Pope Benedict XVI would have found no ground for *Summorum Pontificum*, his famous letter liberating the celebration of the Tridentine Mass. Without Lefebvre's intransigence, the Roman Rite almost certainly would have disappeared without a trace in the atmosphere of anti-traditional persecution. For the Roman Rite was repressed without mercy, and that repression, supposedly in the service of a new, "open" Church, was made possible by a final surge of the centralized power of the papacy that characterized the Church prior to the council and is no longer possible—another irony of that era. Protests by the faithful and by priests were dismissed and handled contemptuously. The Catholic Church in the twentieth century showed no more odious face than in the persecution of the ancient rite that had, until that time, given the Church her identifiable form. The prohibition of the rite was accomplished with iconoclastic fury in countless churches. Those years saw the desecration of places of worship, the tearing down of altars, the tumbling of statues, and the scrapping of precious vestments.

If you cannot abide the disobedience of Archbishop Lefebvre—because it is more than a little sinister that something redemptive for the Church should arise directly from the grievous sin of disobedience to ecclesiastical authority—you may comfort yourself with the thought that his act of conscious disobedience on the particular point of the Roman Rite was not that at all. When Pope Benedict had the greatness of soul to issue *Summorum Pontificum*, he not only reintroduced the Roman Rite into the liturgy of the Church but declared that it had never been forbidden, because it could never be forbidden. No pope and no council possess the authority to invalidate, abolish, or forbid a rite that is so deeply rooted in the history of the Church.

Not only the liberal and Protestant enemies of the Roman Rite but also its defenders, who in a decades-long struggle had begun to give up hope, could barely contain their astonishment. Everyone still had the strict prohibitions of countless bishops echoing in their ears, threats of excommunication and subtle accusations. And one hardly dared draw the conclusion that, in view of Pope Benedict's correcting of the wrongful suppression of the Roman Rite, Blessed Pope Paul VI had apparently been in error when he expressed his strong conviction that the rite long entrusted to the Church should never again be celebrated anywhere in the world. Benedict XVI did even more: He explained that there was only a single Roman Rite which possesses two forms, one "ordinary" and the other "extraordinary"—the latter term referring to the traditional rite. In this way, the traditional form was made the standard for the newly revised form. The pope expressed the wish that the two forms should mutually fructify and enrich each other. It is therefore natural to assume that the new rite, with its great flexibility and many possible forms of celebration, must draw near to the older, steady, and fixed form of the Roman

Subversive Catholicism

Rite, which provides no latitude whatsoever for encroachments or modifications of any kind. According to the approach stipulated by Benedict's letter, the celebrant of the new form of the rite is even required to celebrate the Mass in both forms, and must do so with the same spirit if he does not want to contradict the truth that he is dealing with a single rite in two forms.

* * *

WHENEVER Pope Benedict spoke of a mutual influence and enrichment between the two forms of the rite, he surely did so with an ulterior motive. He believed in organic development in the area of liturgy. He condemned the revolution in the liturgy that coincided with the revolutionary year 1968, and he saw the connection between the liturgical revolution and the cultural one in world-historical terms, for both contradict the ideal of organic evolution and development. He regarded it as a serious offense against the spirit of the Church that the peremptory order of a pope should be taken as warrant to encroach upon the collective heritage of all preceding generations. After decades of use throughout the world, Benedict not only considered it a practical impossibility simply to prohibit the new rite with its serious flaws, but in all likelihood he also perceived that such an act, even if it had been feasible, would have continued along the erroneous path taken by his predecessor, one of reform by fiat. The correct path would be found, so he hoped, in a gradual growing together of the old and new forms, a process to be encouraged and gently fostered by the pope.

This hope of restored liturgical continuity was connected to the concept of a "reform of the reform," a notion Benedict had already introduced when he was a cardinal. What Ratzinger wished to encourage with the idea of a reform of the reform is exactly what the council fathers at Vatican II had in mind when they formulated *Sacrosanctum Concilium*, the Constitution on the Sacred Liturgy. They wanted to allow exceptions to the use of Latin as the common language of the liturgy, insofar as it should be beneficial to the salvation of souls. That the vernacular was presented as the exception only emphasized the immense significance of Latin as the language of the Church. They imagined a certain streamlining of the rite, such as the elimination of the preparatory prayer at the steps of the altar and the closing Gospel reading, which would have been highly lamentable losses without any noteworthy advantages, but which would not have damaged the essence of the liturgy. Of course they left the ancient *offertorium* untouched. These prayers over the bread and wine make clear the priestly and sacrificial character of the Mass and are therefore essential. Among these, the *epiclesis*, the invocation of the Holy Spirit who will consecrate the offerings, is especially important. According to the apostolic tradition, which includes the Eastern Roman Empire, this prayer of consecration is critical.

There can be no question that the council fathers regarded the Roman Canon as absolutely binding. The celebration of the liturgy *ad orientem*, facing eastward to the Lord who is coming again, was also uncontested by the majority of council fathers. Even those who undertook the Pauline reform of the Mass and who swept aside the will of the council fathers didn't dare touch this ancient and continuous practice. It was the spirit of the 1968 revolution that gained control of the liturgy and removed the worship of God from the center of the Catholic rite, installing in its place a clerical-instructional interaction between the priest and the congregation. The council fathers also desired no change in the tradition of church music. It is with downright incredulity that one reads these and other passages of the Constitution on the Sacred Liturgy, for their plain sense was given exactly the opposite meaning by the enthusiastic defenders of post-conciliar "development." One cannot say that Ratzinger's call for a reform of the reform intended in any way to go back "behind the council," as the antagonists of Pope Benedict have maintained. As any fair-minded reading of *Sacrosanctum Concilium* makes clear, the reform of the reform has no goal other than realizing the agenda of the council.

Pope Benedict proceeded very carefully. He pursued his plan through general remarks and observations. While still a cardinal, he let it be known that the demand for celebration of the Eucharist *versus populum*, facing the congregation, is based in error. He endorsed the scholarly work of the theologian Klaus Gamber, who provided proof that never in her history, aside from a very few exceptions, had the Church celebrated the liturgy facing the congregation. Ratzinger pleaded that, if it is impossible for the altar to be turned around, priests should place a large crucifix on the altar so that they can face it during the prayers of consecration. He fought with varying success for the correction of the words of institution that, with the introduction of the vernacular, had been falsely translated in many places. For example, in contradiction to the wording of the Greek text, one hears from the altar that Christ had offered the chalice of his blood "for all" (a reprehensible presumption of salvation) instead of the correct phrase "for many." In Germany, the land of the Reformation that most strenuously resisted Ratzinger, the erroneous translation remains uncorrected to this day.

Other attempts at a reform of the reform might have followed these, but all would have had slim chance of success. One of the most important consequences of the Second Vatican Council has been the destruction of the organizational structure of the Church by the introduction of national bishops' conferences, something entirely alien to classical canon law. This diminishes the direct relationship of each individual bishop to the pope; every Vatican intervention in local abuses shatters when it hits the concrete wall of the respective bishops' conference. This is what happened recently when the prefect of the Congregation for Divine Worship called for a return to the celebration of the Eucharist *ad orientem*. After an outcry of indignation, mainly from English clerics, the request, which was entirely justified, had to be dropped immediately.

Pope Benedict himself undertook no further attempts in this direction. One may well say that he gave up his deeply felt desire for a reform of the reform when he arrived at the decision, in its essence still puzzling, to abdicate. He must have known that few in positions of power in the uppermost reaches of the Church's hierarchy had pursued the reform of the reform with the same conviction as he did. When he withdrew, he effectively gave up this project. He then had to witness his successor, far from shying away from the issue, actually condemning in quite explicit terms any thought of a reform of the reform. Therefore the greatest achievement of Pope Benedict, at least in a liturgical sense, will remain *Summorum Pontificum*. With this instrument he accorded the Roman Rite a secure place in the life of the Church, one protected by canon law.

Anyone who thinks that this does not amount to much is simply unaware of the long decades that preceded these official documents. They were, to use the words of Friedrich Hölderlin, "leaden times." No one who has a clear picture of the state of the present Church and of the world in general could hope that a single pope, during a single pontificate, would be able to correct the defective liturgical development that was encouraged by a mentality antagonistic to spiritual realities. But everyone who worked to keep the Roman Rite alive was aware of the endless obstacles placed in their path. These obstacles have not disappeared everywhere, but it is impossible to ignore the great difference *Summorum Pontificum* has made. The places where the Tridentine Mass is celebrated today have multiplied. The traditional Roman Rite can now be celebrated in proper churches, which causes many people to forget the cellars and courtyards where those who loved the ancient rite long maintained a fugitive existence. The number of young priests with a love for the Tridentine Mass has increased considerably, as has the number of older priests who have begun to learn it. More and more bishops are prepared to celebrate confirmation and holy orders according to the old rite.

These facts may give little comfort to those who have the misfortune to live in a country where this renewal of the ancient form is nowhere to be seen—and there are more than enough such regions. The time has come to set aside a widespread assumption in the Catholic Church that the liturgy and religious education are in good hands with the clergy. This encourages passivity among the faithful, who believe that they do not have to concern themselves with these matters. This is not so. The great liturgical crisis following the Second Vatican Council, which was part of a larger crisis of faith and authority, put an end to the illusion that the laity need not be involved. We now have a duty to participate in and promote a faithful recovery of the apostolic tradition in all its rich abundance.

* * *

THE NOW decades-old movement for the restoration of the Roman Rite has been to a considerable extent a lay movement. The position of priests who support the Roman Rite was and will be strengthened by *Summorum Pontificum*, and hopefully the cause of the Tridentine Mass will receive further support from the eagerly awaited reconciliation of the Society of St. Pius X with the Holy See. Yet this does not change the fact that it will be the laity who will be decisive in bringing about the success of efforts to reform the reform. The laity of today differs from the laity of forty years ago. They had precise knowledge of the Roman Rite and took its loss bitterly and contested it. The young people who are turning to the Roman Rite today often did not know it as children. They are not, as Pope Francis erroneously presumes, nostalgically longing for a lost time. On the contrary, they are experiencing the Roman Rite as something new. It opens an entire world to them, the exploration of which promises to be inexhaustibly fascinating. It is true that those who discover the Roman Rite today and relish its formal exactness and rigorous orthodoxy are naturally an elite group, yet not in a social sense. Theirs is a higher mystical receptivity and an aesthetic sensitivity to the difference between truth and falsehood. As Johan Huizinga, author of *The Waning of the Middle Ages*, established nearly a century ago, there exists a close connection between orthodoxy and an appreciation of style.

The Fate of the Rite is the Fate of the Church

The vast majority of the faithful have in the meantime never known anything else but the revised Mass in its countless manifestations. They have lost any sense of the spiritual wealth of the Church and in many cases simply are not capable of following the old rite. They should not be criticized on account of this. The Tridentine Mass demands a lifetime of education, and the postconciliar age is characterized, among other things, by the widespread abandonment of religious instruction. The Catholic religion with its high number of believers has actually become the most unknown religion in the world, especially to its own adherents. While there are many Catholics who feel repelled and offended by the superficiality of the new rite as it is frequently celebrated today, by the odious music, the puritanical kitsch, the trivialization of dogma, and the profane character of new church buildings, the gap that has opened up in the forty years between the traditional rite and the new Mass is very deep, often unbridgeable. The challenge becomes more difficult because one of the peculiarities of the old rite is that it makes itself accessible only slowly—unless the uninitiated newcomer to this ancient pattern of worship is a religious genius. One has never "learned everything there is to learn" about the Roman Rite, because in its very origin and essence this enduring and truly extraordinary form is hermetic, presupposing arcane discipline and rigorous initiation.

If the Tridentine Mass is to prosper, the ground must be prepared for a new generation to receive such an initiation. Pope Benedict disappointed many advocates of the old liturgy because he did not do more for them. He refused the urgent requests to celebrate the Latin Mass at least once as pope, something he had occasionally done while a cardinal. But this refusal stems from the fact that he believed—no matter how welcome such a celebration would have been—that the reinstitution of the old rite, like all significant movements in the history of the Church, must come from below, not as a result of a papal decree from above. In the meantime, the post-conciliar work of destruction has wounded multitudes of the faithful. Unless a change of mind and a desire for a return to the sacred begin to sprout in countless individual hearts, administrative actions by Rome, however well-intentioned and sound, can effect little.

Summorum Pontificum makes priests and the laity responsible for the Roman Rite's future—if it means a lot to them. It is up to them to celebrate it in as many places as possible, to win over for it as many people as possible, and to disseminate the arcane knowledge concerning its sacred mysteries. The odium of disobedience and defiance against the Holy See has been spared them by Pope Benedict's promulgation, and they are making use of the right granted them by the Church's highest legislator, but this right only has substance if it is claimed and used. The law is there. No Catholic can, as was possible not long ago, contend that fostering the Roman Rite runs counter to the will of the Church.

Perhaps it is even good that, despite *Summorum Pontificum*, the Tridentine Mass is still not promoted by the great majority of bishops. If it is a true treasure without which the Church would not be itself, then it will not be won until it has been fought for. Its loss was a spiritual catastrophe for the Church and had disastrous consequences far beyond the liturgy, and that loss can only be overcome by a widespread spiritual renewal. It is not necessarily a bad thing that members of the hierarchy, in open disobedience to *Summorum Pontificum*, continue to put obstacles in the way of champions of the Roman Rite. As we learn in the lives of the saints and the orders they founded, the established authorities typically persecute with extreme mistrust new movements and attempt to suppress them. This is one of the constants of church history, and it characterizes every unusual spiritual effort, indeed, every true reform, for true reform consists of putting on the bridle, of returning to a stricter order. This is the trial by fire that all reformers worthy of their name had to endure. The Roman Rite will be won back in hundreds of small chapels, in improvised circumstances throughout the whole world, celebrated by

The Fate of the Rite is the Fate of the Church

young priests with congregations that have many small children, or it will not be won back at all.

Recapturing the fullness of the Church's liturgy is now a matter for the young. Those who experienced the abolition and uncanonical proscription of the old rite in the late 1960s were formed by the liturgical praxis of the 1950s and the decades prior. It may sound surprising, but this praxis was not the best in many countries. The revolution that was to disfigure the Mass cast a long shadow ahead of itself. In many cases, the liturgical practice was such that people no longer believed in the mystagogical power of the rite. In many countries, the liturgical architecture of the rite was obscured or even dismantled. There were silent Masses during which a prayer leader incessantly recited prayers in the vernacular that were not always translations of the Latin prayers, and in a number of places Gregorian chant played a subordinate role. Those who are twenty or thirty today have no bad habits of these sorts. They can experience the rite in its new purity, free of the incrustations of the more recent past.

The great damage caused by the liturgical revolution after Vatican II consists above all in the way in which the Church lost the conviction with which all Catholics—illiterate goatherds, maids and laborers, Descartes and Pascal—naturally took part in the Church's sacred worship. Up until then, the rite was among the riches of the poor, who, through it, entered into a world that was otherwise closed to them. They experienced in the old Mass the life to come as well as life in the present, an experience of which only artists and mystics are otherwise capable. This loss of shared transcendence available to the most humble cannot be repaired for generations, and this great loss is what makes the ill-considered reform of the Mass so reprehensible. It is a moral outrage that those who gutted the Roman Rite because of their presumption and delusion were permitted to rob a future generation of their full Catholic inheritance. Yet it is now at least possible for individuals and for small groups to gradually win back a modicum of un-self-conscious familiarity with even the most arcane prayers of the Church. Today, children can grow into the rite and thus attain a new, more advanced level of spiritual participation.

The movement for the old rite, far from indicating aesthetic self-satisfaction, has, in truth, an apostolic character. It has been observed that the Roman Rite has an especially strong effect on converts, indeed, that it has even brought about a considerable number of conversions. Its deep rootedness in history and its alignment with the end of the world create a sacred time antithetical to the present, a present that, with its acquisitive preoccupations, leaves many people unsatisfied. Above all, the old rite runs counter to the faith in progress that has long gone hand in hand with an economic mentality that is now curdling into anxiety regarding the future and even a certain pessimism. This contradiction with the spirit of our present age should not be lamented. It betokens, rather, a general awakening from a two-hundred-year-old delusion. Christians always knew that the world fell because of original sin and that, as far as the course of history is concerned, it offers no reason at all for optimism. The Catholic religion is, in the words of T. S. Eliot, a "philosophy of disillusionment" that does not suppress hope, but rather teaches us not to direct our hope toward something that the world cannot give. The liturgy of Rome and, naturally, Greek Orthodoxy's Divine Liturgy of St. John Chrysostom open a window that draws our gaze from time into eternity.

Reform is a return to form. The movement that seeks to restore the form of the Latin Rite is still an avant-garde, attracting young people who find modern society suffocating. But it can only be a truly Christian avant-garde if it does not forget those it leads into battle; it must not forget the multitude who will someday have to find their way back into the abundant richness of the Catholic religion, once the generations who, in the wake of the Second Vatican Council, sought the salvation of the Church in its secularization have sunk into their graves.

Rome, Third Sunday of Advent,
"Gaudete," 2016

PART III

Christians in the World

God Must Be in Europe's Constitution

WHICH GOD is it supposed to be, exactly, that the European constitution—in accordance with the wishes of certain Catholic states and those parties which call themselves Christian—ought to refer? When, after the murderous wars of religion, Thomas Hobbes developed his doctrine of a state that stands above the religions, the minimal formula which he thought all citizens ought to profess—regardless of the particular confession to which they might belong—was "that Jesus is the Christ." Could even this minimal profession attain a majority today? Probably not.

In the Protestant theology of the twentieth century, and that of Catholics since the Second Vatican Council, the view would be, rather, that "Jesus is no longer the Christ." For the greater majority of modern theologians Jesus is, at best, a godly man who suffered unjustly: this doctrine has found its way into the broadest circle of the Christian population and represents—totally independent of the still tradition-bound statements of the pope—their view of the person of Jesus. After its great popularization in the fourth century, Arianism is again in the twentieth century the prevailing theological movement. Regardless of how one stands in regard to this situation, Arianism is not Christian. Christianity acknowledges in Christ the anointed one, the Son of God, God Himself. How many Christian politicians, who today promote a reference to Christianity in the European constitution, are Christians in this sense? Or ought Christianity only find access into the constitutional charter as a cultural institution? It is indisputable that Christianity was the most significant factor in the development of the modern European states—even those developments which have taken place in the teeth of Christianity and the Church are due, in reality and with seamless causality, to the Christian religion. If we have a clear view that free states based upon the rule of law succeed, and have succeeded, only in those places where a Christian and feudal past have predisposed a relationship between law and freedom, it would seem appropriate, and an act of gratitude, to acknowledge within the constitution the historical preconditions for what has been achieved. Constitutions, however, are not history books. They are a catalogue of the rights and duties of the subjects of that constitution. Historical memories, imprecise philosophies, the proclamation of notorious "values"—which are simultaneously both more and less than concrete rights—have nothing to do with constitutions. One ought not forget that Christianity did not unfurl its enormous impact upon the European states as a vague system of values or as a cultural atmosphere, but rather as a legal order of an immediately binding nature. What sort of enforceable claim could result from a general acknowledgement of Christianity, within the constitution, as a power that had once shaped Europe? None? Then this embellishment can be safely dispensed with.

Now the "God" who might end up in the European constitution, and who receives a mention in the German Constitution, is nonetheless probably not the Trinitarian God of Christianity, but rather more a God like that in Lessing's play *Nathan the Wise*, fairly distant and fairly unknown, "that higher being whom we venerate"—as Heinrich Böll put it in his radio satire. God, the friend of the good and enemy of the bad. As scary as it may be for the political friends of God, they will not be able to get around even so attenuated a theological statement about God as that—God, whom they wish to empower, in order that He might empower them. If not Jesus as the incarnate God, does God at least still have a chance in Europe as the creator of heaven and earth, revealing the Ten Commandments and founding the moral law, as the judge of the world who helps the oppressed to victory, *sub specie aeternitatis* (Latin: "from the point of view of eternity")? And what could such a God—the

God of Abraham, Isaac and Jacob, who is also, by the way, the God of Islam—contribute to a constitution which knows itself to be in His debt?

Few people are aware that the first constitutions of Europe, reaching back into the early Middle Ages, were monarchies of "divine right." Nowadays people like to interpret the "divine right" of European kings as an indication of arrogance and high-handedness; in reality, however, it was a sign of the subordination of the ruler to the Ten Commandments and the Gospel. That the king ruled "by divine right" and not by his own right signified a restriction of his power and a limitation of force. In this early form, the mentioning of God was identical to the essence of the constitution—to every type of constitution. "If God does not exist, everything is permitted," runs a key sentence in Dostoyevsky's *Brothers Karamazov*, often heatedly contested but never refuted. To call upon God in the constitution is the self-restriction of a political system which will not allow itself to do everything of which it is capable.

The God of the Ten Commandments, who requires that there be no other gods beside Him, also prohibits the divinization of the state and society, which were first allowed to experience their fullest development in the twentieth century. The invocation of the God of the Ten Commandments in a constitution confirms that the fundamentals of law can never be the creation of society, or of a law maker or of an impressive majority, but are rather pre-ordained and cannot be altered by the decisions of a majority. The invocation of God in the constitution implies an avowal of the idea that the state cannot create the law, but is rather only called to protect it; indeed, that the state only possesses legitimacy so long as it guards the law that was not created by it. Wherever God has been named in constitutions, the purpose behind it was to bring the principle of the rule of law to expression. Law, in the sense of the rule of law, is something before which not only the individual but even the state must bow. One does not, however, bow before something one has created oneself. This has never meant, of course, that the law was not trampled underfoot in states which derived their legitimacy from God. Yet that cannot diminish the weight of such a reference to God. No morality should be judged by whether those who espouse it actually adhere to it: what is important is to ask why people have an uneasy conscience—no system of values can claim to do more than call forth a guilty conscience.

However, the acknowledgement of God in the constitution is also an acknowledgement of history. To have God in the constitution means that justice does not begin with democracy or European unification, but rather has existed in the world since God revealed it. To have God in the constitution is an element of modesty which it would be well for such an oppressive institution—as a European government necessarily must be—to have. To have God in the constitution would be as if to say that the goal of history is not the unification of Europe, but rather that such a step is but one stop along man's path through time. With God in the constitution the developing super-state admits that it is not perfect, and that it cannot be perfect. The reference to God is simultaneously the hole in the air balloon, out of which the gas of conceit and self-overestimation can escape. In this regard even atheists, for whom an effective self-restriction of the state is also opportune, have to agree with the view of the Enlightenment: "If God did not exist, man would have to invent Him."

The Anarchism of Mercy

Justice? "Social justice" is the concept upon which the German welfare state is based. In a state in which, following the principles of Confucius or Plato, the exactitude of terminology ought to be closely guarded, the term "social justice" would have to be banned. It is suspicious already that the talk is of "justice" and not of "law." Justice is a big word for a big, indeed lofty, matter; it is a characteristic of God ("righteousness" is the word used in the King James Bible) and that takes it beyond the realm of definition, for it is something that will surprise men on the last day. As the hymn says, "Earthly justice, Lord, betrayed you…" Used politically, the talk of justice has an almost demagogic character: it expresses both something more and something else than "law." Naturally a state can create a law according to which each citizen, in time of need, is entitled to receive assistance, but it makes no sense that "justice" is supposed to undergird this law. It hardly requires explanation to show how advantageous it is, for every state, that each of its citizens should be protected from the most extreme hardship. An economy based upon mass consumption requires masses of consumers; a nation is secure only when it does not include substantial groups that have nothing to lose; such a nation is spared the occasional, uncontrollable political tensions between the haves and the have-nots. These are solid grounds for a generous system of social security—because they do not require recourse to "justice," which, by the way, can also be used very effectively to argue *against* our social security system. Why is it "just" that someone who will do nothing to maintain his own life is protected from falling into the abyss? "Let not the lazy belly squander / what others' diligence has won…," wrote Heinrich Heine in his interpretation of "social justice." Certainly, by the "lazy belly" Heine did not have in mind the recipients of transfer payments, yet the verse could equally be applied to them, for the notion of "justice" cannot be pinned down, but can turn up in contexts that reveal its inadequacy.

Just as dubious as the association with "social justice" is the attempt to anchor the principle of social welfare in the catalogue of constitutional rights. It is the most ramshackle states of the world—particularly in Latin America—that can give a proud list of constitutional rights: rights to work and education and other wonderful things. Yet rights which the state does not have the power to enforce are no rights at all, and they allow the concept of "rights" itself to become an object of mockery. The point at which a state will no longer have the financial capability to come to the aid of its poor is constantly debated; but that such a point exists *cannot be denied*. The same politicians who, in public, talk of a secure pension, admit in private that Germany, for instance, is bankrupt. "Where there is nothing, the emperor has lost his rights," runs the old saying. Ought it also be applied to those who receive the pension?

"Mercy" (*misericordia*, "compassion") is suggested as the principle by which the state is obliged to help the needy. Now, *misericordia* is a virtue defined by religion, and those who "show mercy"—according to religion—can only be individual people, never an institution. Even the right of the Federal German President to pardon a condemned criminal can, with good reason, be questioned: the king can be clement, the dispensation of clemency is even a characteristic of kingship, but an elected representative of the people does not actually possess the legitimacy to grant clemency and thereby play the king. Democracy, by its very nature, is *merciless*, mercy-less: the capricious disregarding of the law that the state itself has created is, strictly speaking, forbidden by it. Given how little the principle of mercy suits the democratic state it would seem, by its very definition, to be diametrically opposed to state action: mercy, by contrast, is that element of anarchy which the Christian—as a loyal citizen—constantly reserves to himself. The merciful man realizes that he *does not simply stand under one law*. His conviction is that neither the state nor society have the tools to solve all the conflicts of life in society. In order to be merciful, he is even prepared to breach civil laws and bear the consequences.

The "anti-social" character of Christian mercy is also displayed in the fact that the beneficiary of this virtue is not, actually, the person who is helped by it, but rather *the person who is merciful*. It is the souls of the rich that are meant to be saved by the virtue of mercy; the glowing fire of mercy ought to melt the icy crust of avarice, self-righteousness, and aggression which surrounds the souls of the wealthy. It is not the problem of poverty that Christianity wishes to solve—"you will always have the poor with you"—but rather, Christianity wishes to open people's eyes to the fact that the poor man is one manifestation of the incarnate God. It is clear that Christian standards are not suited for the foundation of a state—but it is equally clear that it is much to the benefit of a state built upon law when many of its citizens are Christians.

In order to comprehend our welfare state it is important to hold in mind the unbridgeable difference between the North American democracy and European democracies. The North American democracy truly does rest upon a—still only fictional—Rousseau-style "social contract." According to this theory, equal citizens have come together to agree upon certain common institutions which are meant to guarantee each of them a life to be lived according to the concept of individualism. This concept was first called into question when those groups who were not part of this contract—African Americans and Latinos—acquired stronger political clout.

The European states took a completely different path. The legal concept of sovereignty was decisive for their formation as states, a concept that was created for the Baroque monarchs. The monarch, as the sovereign, *was* the state and it was the duty of the citizen to maintain the sovereign. Germany, as everyone knows, had a great many sovereigns—thousands at one time or another—and this probably made it easier for our people to imagine the sovereign with innumerable heads, like the famous frontispiece of Hobbes's *Leviathan*, on which the figure of the crowned sovereign is formed by many tiny figures of men.

With the fall of the monarchies in Germany and the installation of democracy, the entire populace did indeed come forward in place of the sovereign. Every voter received his sixty-millionth portion of sovereignty, with the corresponding right to sustentation. The guarantee of a generously proportioned minimum of existence for every elector is nothing other than the appanage which was once paid to members of the royal family. It has nothing to do with the elevated idea of justice, nor with the even more elevated notion of mercy, and absolutely *nothing* to do with human rights that are promised—in unenforceable generosity—to every man on earth. It is the very purpose of the state to maintain the sovereign; that was true of Louis XIV and it is true of the "sovereign" of the German Republic, i.e., the German people.

What happens, then, when the state revenues no longer extend to providing appanages to increasing numbers of sustentation-needy people who embody the sovereignty? We know how inclement sovereigns were once the means no longer flowed; Colbert wisely stayed silent when Louis XIV furrowed his brows; and the governors of the democratic "sovereign" (the "great boor") are inclined to even greater caution. The governors know that it is pointless to suggest economizations to the sovereign, for they themselves would be instantly replaced. The only means they possess of reducing the ever more absurd burden of debt is inflation and subsequent currency reform; such an event will be seen as a natural catastrophe, with no one to blame. The class which really has to suffer under such treatment, that is, the independent folk who are saving for their old age, is so small and of such political insignificance that their cry can be easily ignored.

Because of all this, the careful attempts of the European

bureaucracy to diminish and dilute the sovereignty of the people ought to attract attention. No one would ever express the idea of taking away the voting rights of citizens, but quietly stripping that right of any value—that, it seems, is being attempted in one form or another. Referendums have had bad press of late: we want the decision of the majority, of course!—but it must be the *correct* one. The basic existential law of every form of state, including democracy, is determined by whether it can create legitimacy; yet among the elite spheres of specialists in Brussels they are toying with the idea of a legitimacy that would be out of range of democratic control. Incidentally, Chancellor Angela Merkel is supposed to have been very put out by the judgment of the Karlsruhe Justices on the Lisbon Treaty. All diminutions of German sovereignty by which it is further subjected to the control of Brussels "would further weaken the influence of Germany" and is a policy no longer in tune with the times.

A diminished sovereignty of the people, however, would also have a looser grip upon state finances; a voter whose vote has been devalued has just as little capacity to apply pressure as a constitutional monarch. If, one day, it happens to reach such a point, many people would once again find it rather important to live in a nation with a large proportion of faithful Christians.

On the Value of Proscription[1]

SHOULD THE German state have a genuine interest in banning blasphemy in art and in published media, and in enforcing this ban by punishment? One could hold the position that the secular state, which regards itself as neutral in the face of the religions and anti-religions of its citizens, is condemned to silence on the question of blasphemy. Such a thing does not exist, it is said, for this kind of state; no more can it arbitrate in a dispute about the weather, which would involve insulting the sun and moon—although, of course, if it came to showering abuse on meteorologists, the state would have to ensure that the line of insult and defamation were not overstepped. It can be questioned, however, whether the Federal Republic of Germany is actually such a neutral state as regards its worldview. If the constitution is examined, the answer becomes simple: the constitution, according to its preamble, is formulated "conscious of responsibility before God and man." The question as to which God the fathers and mothers of this constitutional work had in mind, is equally easy to answer: it was the God of Christianity—at the end of the 1940s it would have been difficult to think of any other.

This is not the place for a detailed investigation of the ways in which the principles of the liberal state based on law—which the Federal Republic wishes to be—has emerged from the commandments of Christianity, even in those instances when, in conflict with those commandments, it appeared to want to find

---

1. Discussion paper delivered at the conference "Is This Acceptable? Art and Its Limits" (Culture Institute, Essen, Germany).

itself in opposition to Christianity. Article 1 of the Constitution alone, which concerns the dignity of man, is inconceivable without Christian inspiration. The fact that the nature of dignity cannot be lost—its *character indelibilis*—is a specifically Christian proposition.

The famous Böckenförde-Formula—the bourgeois-liberal state rests upon presuppositions that it can neither create nor guarantee—has in mind the fact that even the Federal Republic did not spring whole and entire from the head of Zeus, but rather rests upon presuppositions which arose in other contexts. These presuppositions—which were created neither by the Federal Republic nor by its lawmakers, yet are nonetheless built into the foundation of the edifice of the state—must, so long as this constitution is valid, in principle stand under the particular protection of the state. It has an interest in its constitution not being intellectually eroded and shriveled into empty formulae: it should remain a living reality. It is on this point that there could be based an obligation of the state to protect that God—upon whose commandments the state wishes to construct its moral order—from blasphemy and insult, which would in time denude that moral order of respect.

This does not mean that the societal changes of recent decades have not impaired, to put it mildly, the idea of the religious affiliation of the constitution: if a constitution such as the basic law requires were to be newly written today, it might no longer include this reference to God. The question, however, is hypothetical: there will be no new constitution in the long term. All of the essential political forces are united on this point.

Yet even for a state which is strictly neutral regarding worldviews, the necessity of a fight against blasphemy could well arise if the state order were thereby endangered. This could happen if a large group of believers felt themselves so harmed by blasphemy in their religious convictions that their anger were to become a public problem. This question touches upon a principle of all statehood: the monopoly of force possessed by the state. This monopoly rests upon the relationship between pro-

On the Value of Proscription

tection and obedience: the citizen cedes to the state the implementation (by force of arms) of his honor and rights and is obedient to the prohibition of violence. In return he gains the protection of the state. When a sufficiently large group no longer feel themselves protected in their religious convictions by the state, this relationship runs into danger.

For a long time this appeared to be only a theoretical question. The Christians of Germany had, in overwhelming majority, lost their interest in religious issues; what was often termed tolerance was, for the most part, nothing more than pure indifference. The depiction of the Christian religion in schools and in the media portrays Christianity as a violence-filled ideology which threatens freedom; Baudelaire's dictum that Voltaire was the "prédicateur des concierges," the janitor's preacher, also applies to that intellectual milieu within the Federal Republic—where the name of Voltaire is never heard. Today the majority opinion holds that Christians are basically obliged to accept insults to their confession without complaint. Atheists with sketchy knowledge of the Bible demand that Christians, in the face of blasphemy, "turn the other cheek" in accordance with the commandment of their master. Despite all this, on the Christian side there is still no protest. Even bishops look bashfully aside when the talk is of blasphemy; they simply do not want to notice it—or they might have to take up a position in regard to it.

Now that a strong Islamic minority has taken up residence in Germany, this idea has again suddenly gained impetus. Unexpectedly, the champions of integration within the German political parties find themselves confronted with people for whom blasphemy is no laughing matter. By the demand for tolerance the latter primarily mean that non-Muslims in Germany should respect the Islamic faith and treat it with the due reverence appropriate even for those who do not share that faith. In England the maintenance of public order required that the film *The Last Temptation of Christ* by Martin Scorsese be banned, following mass demonstrations by the

Subversive Catholicism

Muslim community over the insults accorded to the prophet Isa (Jesus). Yet even in Germany a legal proscription of blasphemy, in the face of a growing German Islam, may once again gain traction.

Is the threat of censorship and punishment in the case of blasphemy a threat to art? The Federal Republic, in contrast to other European nations, wished to institute in the constitution, alongside the guarantees of the freedom of opinion and press, a "freedom of art"—a guarantee which appeared questionable to many in the legal world, as this freedom is already sufficiently protected by the freedoms of opinion and the press. Furthermore, claiming this freedom before a court would always require an examination as to whether in the disputed instance it was truly a work of art, a question which—in our current state in the history of ideas—a court is no longer able to answer. It would also be suggesting that, in this one instance, the case should be argued from the point of view of the artist and not that of law. Despite the demands for unrestricted freedom—urgently claimed by artists—the restriction of this very freedom has been highly beneficial for the development of art throughout its historical development. Not being able to say everything, to be surrounded by rigid regulations, has principally had an incendiary effect upon the fantasy of artists and inspired them to the boldest of solutions; the saying that "censorship refines style" is famous, as is the maxim of Karl Kraus, who personally experienced a great deal of censorship: "Any sentence understood by the censor would be justly banned."

Today, blasphemy that is not directed against the prophet Mohammed is completely without risk. The attempts to push the boundaries in blasphemy—involving the covert hope that such a thing, despite all previous experience, might still lead to a scandal or a success-promoting ban—devolve into nothingness. Vulgarity acquires a particularly stale aftertaste because, in its self-righteousness and gross self-display, it simply repels the public. The story is told of Jean-Jacques Rousseau that one day he encountered a mocking libertine spouting blasphemies; he brought the gentleman to silence with the following words: "If it is dastardly to remain silent when bad things are being spoken of absent friends, it is all the more shabby to remain silent when the same occurs of God, who is present." Here we have the serious tone that is appropriate to the topic of blasphemy. Blasphemy as a "cool" pose or as calculated foolery is cheap and cowardly, and its artistic contribution remains accordingly limited. It is probably hopeless at the present time to appeal to the taste of artists who delight in blasphemy; hopeless to appeal to the instinctive reluctance to harming the defenseless. These bold "blasphemers" are happy to cry "Victory!" as they run through gates that are wide open anyway; they perform in a jaded and blasé milieu, and act as though they had just risked the pyre of the Inquisition. For myself, I am incapable of any sense of outrage when Muslims, insulted in their faith, administer a violent shock to blasphemous "artists"—if they can be so called. I welcome the fact, if it means that there are once again in our world people like Jean-Jacques Rousseau, for whom God is present. It will do a lot for the social climate if blasphemy once more becomes dangerous.

The claim of the artist to freedom is total and countenances not even the slightest restriction. Yet this claim is not directed against the state and society, but rather against the artist himself. What he must struggle against are the shears within his own head; that readiness to serve the expectations of society, to trim his thoughts according to fashion; the desire to please, to accord with current trends, not to get too far away from the *consensus omnium*. He must write what angel or devil, muses or demons, dictate to his unconscious and whisper in his dreams. But this is the proviso: freedom, for the artist, is not a right or a bundle of rights. Freedom is a characteristic of his personality, which it has created through a life of self-examination. It may well be that this freedom collides with the conceptions of society. It may come to pass that for this—his freedom—the artist must pay a very high price.

I am convinced that the truly free artist happily pays this

price. For him, it goes without saying: society and personal freedom are not always able to accord with one another. The law cannot regulate every circumstance of life. There are collisions, the results of unavoidable conflicts. It is part of the artist's pride and honor that, in the encounter with the legal order—if it has to come to that as a result of his art—he does not complain and call for the courts to intervene. The artist who, for the sake of his art, feels called to injure a social convention, or the belief of those for whom God is present, or even a law, is obliged—and I am convinced of this—to follow that call. He will generously pay the large costs thereby incurred, even if they endanger his existence. The risks which he assumes in his infringement of the law will at the same time, however, protect him from being flippant in practice. In his studio or study he will ask himself: is this blasphemous element really necessary, is it an irreplaceable part of my work—or is it just a flourish, a caprice or piece of insolence? Must I undertake this hazard if I wish to be able to look myself in the mirror?

These questions will be to the benefit of the work. And a work which has come into existence in this way will not fail to obtain the (sometimes perhaps grudging) respect from sincere believers.

A German Pilgrim in Chartres

It was in France that I learned that I was a German Catholic. It was on one of the large Pentecost pilgrimages from Paris to Chartres; Charles Péguy, the most celebrated poet, essayist, public speaker, and editor of journals of the "Catholic renewal," had initiated this pilgrimage before the First World War. After Vatican II, like so many popular spiritual exercises, it had gone to sleep, only to be revived by the movement for Catholic tradition. In Paris, with its creed of "laicism," it still provokes an unbelieving and occasionally dismayed shaking of heads when the procession of ten thousand pilgrims forms up in front of Notre Dame and sets out on its way through the quiet morning streets. You need to be good on your feet to face the one hundred and twenty kilometers that are to be completed at a spanking pace in three days. On the way people pray and sing; whenever we make a forest break, priests spread out through the company dressed in rochet and violet stole, ready to hear confessions. Solemn High Mass is celebrated in a clearing in one of the most beautiful beech woods of Rambouillet. Then the procession leaves the forest and reaches the wide plain of Chartres. In the distance the cathedral rises out of the cornfields. Seeming endless, the pilgrim procession winds its way toward this sacred spot like an infantry column, all standards flying. This, perhaps, is how the body of soldiers looked, led against the English by Joan of Arc, the mysterious shepherd-girl from Lorraine's Domrémy—this intuition came to me like a lightning flash—and the picture seemed perfectly accompanied, in our "detachment," by the singing of old soldiers' songs, led by a young officer. We sang "Marshal Turenne" and "Sainte Marie, Queen of France," and several of the saints invoked in the litanies. After the Mother of God came the Maid of Orléans,

Subversive Catholicism

King Saint Louis, the Curé of Ars, Saint Solange, and the Little Flower, Saint Thérèse of Lisieux. These French pilgrims lifted their eyes to a God who—was French. Their religion and their culture had become—enviably—identical. There was something all-of-a-piece about it, as if they were able to relax in their religion. It would be wrong to suggest that I felt excluded from among my fellow pilgrims; on the contrary they were most hospitable, and in a spiritual way too: their enthusiasm was catching. But I always had the impression that this Catholicism was somehow more self-confident and—in the most beautifully possible sense—at peace with its own condition. It was not always quarrelling with itself; it did not engage in restless longings. This was something with which I, as a German Catholic, was unfamiliar.

For me, being a Catholic meant being something other, something more, even, than being a German. "Catholic" was the higher-order concept, to which my nationality took second place. Being a Catholic was an important step beyond my being German. Bismarck's *Kulturkampf* ("culture war") warriors accused Catholics of not being loyal subjects of the Prussian King; Catholics allowed themselves mental reservation vis-à-vis the state; they were "ultramontanists" whose loyalty bound them to a monarch beyond the Alps—they owed allegiance to the distant Roman pope. How fitting I found this designation! Surely, would not any German Catholic, given his entire history, have to be "ultramontane"? Was it not ultramontanism to prolong the collapsed West Roman empire under the authority of the German kings? This Carolingian Roman empire, which later was given the qualification "of the German nation," was not a national state: for a long time, because of its weakness and its unwillingness to monopolize power, it was not a state at all. This Roman-German imperial realm, a loose confederation that in many ways rested on juridical fictions, claimed to be the empire of all Christians. Where Catholicism joined forces with a political idea was in Germany, in the form of the Holy Roman Empire, which spread its wings over a family of Christian nations like a mother hen protecting her chicks. How often has this idea been scorned, and how often has cruel history confirmed its powerlessness! This cannot change the fact, however, that there *was* this idea. Ideas prove their vitality and their power to inspire the imagination, not through implementing them—on the contrary, it is often the implementation of political ideas that gives them the coup de grâce. After the Second World War and a process of secularization that was definitive and could not be overturned, three Catholics—two of them, Robert Schuman and Alcide de Gasperi are subjects of a beatification process—once again dreamed the dream of Charlemagne's empire and wanted to commend it to a laicist public by using economic arguments. This too is a strong echo of the old idea of an empire that people have declared dead and gone. It is no wonder that it was precisely the Germans who were enthusiastic about it; and it was not only the fact of having lost the war, but a re-emergence of a political disposition—one might say a gene-based inclination—in favor of a supra-national concept of empire, that lent wings to this idea.

However typical, in the case of Germany, this kind of Catholic ultramontanism and supra-nationalism may be, it cannot be denied that this attitude, unique in European culture, always represented a step too far for many Germans. The "Discordia Germaniae" goes back to the time of Tacitus. From its very first moment of cultural existence my German fatherland was already split in two: one part was a region under Roman colonial rule and the other part was barbarian. At this first moment, when a cultured people—the cultured people par excellence—perceived and described the Germans, the latter were already in the power of the spirit of irreconcilable division and suicidal self-hatred. In every century through history this characteristic was exemplified in new and ever more pitiless forms. A celebrated essay by Carl Schmitt begins, "There is an antipathy towards Rome"; in other words, German Catholic ultramontanism, faithfulness to Rome, was

Subversive Catholicism

always accompanied by a hatred of Rome, a nationalistic self-satisfaction on the part of a section of the German people. Martin Luther's Reformation, which made my country a by-word for civil war, the Thirty Years' War (17th century), the Secularization (culminating in 1803), the *Kulturkampf* under Bismarck, the "Los von Rom" ("Away from Rome") movement that started at the end of the 19th century: these are individual phases of a long development. It was accompanied in the spiritual and intellectual sphere by ever more bitter attacks on the Roman Church by science and philosophy. Rudolf Borchardt, the great Jewish essayist and man of letters, saw the approaching period of Hitler's Nazi party as an outpouring of this antipathy to Rome: "On the whole the German people never really accepted imported European culture; increasingly, to a large extent, they offered it silent resistance.... In secret, hidden away in corners, Germans, individuals and the people as a whole, stubbornly held on to the enraged suspicion that they had been fooled by Christianity and simply plundered and duped by Rome, treated as yokels by the courts, scorned by the medieval Church, regarded as stupid by the learned professions, stripped of nerve by a womanish culture and courtesy, led astray by the cult of mind, ... ultimately betrayed by refined manners, ... and literally ruined by the Empire."

- What is new today is that there is not the same opposition, in large areas of the country, between the Christian parties, Roman Catholics and anti-Roman Protestants, because the greater number of Catholic theologians and official representatives—and particularly the laity—have become passionately hostile to Rome. Postconciliar Catholicism, preoccupied with the ecumenical relationship with Protestants, has now become the spearhead of hostility to Rome. One could even say that, so far, the neo-Catholic antipathy to Rome is the only real achievement of the postconciliar ecumenical movement. The ultramontane, once typical of the German Catholic, has long ago been forced into a minority. Within the Catholic Church in Germany he has no forum and no advocate and, if he is a learned theologian, he has no prospect of a professional post. When a German became successor to St. Peter there was clear potential for aggression. A German pope from the distinguished ultramontane party that people had believed defunct provoked the anti-Roman elements in German Catholicism to come into the open. For me, the pope's visit to Germany had a single historical parallel: the visit of Pope Pius VI to Emperor Joseph II in Vienna in an attempt to persuade the monarch not to go ahead with the dissolution of all the religious houses within his realm. As is well known, the attempt failed, although the emperor, who was indeed involved in plans for a "national church," had to learn on this occasion that Catholicism was not to be had without the papacy. The pope's mere presence won the hearts of the "people," as it was so nicely put, that is, of the little people in town and countryside who came in crowds, much to the emperor's annoyance, to ask the blessing of the Bishop of Rome. Is it very rash of me to hope that the German Church of the twenty-first century, whose representatives have deeply entangled themselves in the ominous "dialogue" that aims at founding a national church, might possibly recover their old ultramontane instinct and show their shepherds that they are prepared to be Catholics only *with* the pope and not against him? Or will Pope Benedict, great patriot that he is, have to recognize that, for a German pope, there is no more foreign and remote land than his German homeland?

A Magical Place: Lourdes and the Pilgrims

The City and the Churches

LIKE A SNUG, old-fashioned spa town Lourdes lies in a green valley through which flows the Gave, a broad mountain stream. Looking down on it from an elevated vantage point, the whole city seems to consist of almshouses and countless hotels from the turn of the century; it is not immediately evident that the ground floor of each and every house in Lourdes is the shopfront of a devotional and religious store. The devotion industry has been around since the time of pilgrimages to pagan places of worship. Diminutive statuettes of the mother goddess could be bought all around the Temple of Diana in Ephesus, and the many voluptuous, rounded balconies of the "Hôtel Moderne"—right next to the holy areas of Lourdes—do truly call to mind the hundred breasts of Diana. Huysmans, who describes Lourdes with a combination of love and revulsion, certainly hated the "Hôtel Moderne." Today the over-decorated building arouses nothing more than sweet nostalgia. One cannot but think of the Black Forest when in Lourdes; a misty humidity, rest cures in a hall that smells of pine, and abundant meal times. The specialty of the region is the duck, "magret de canard" and "confit de canard," and it is to the credit of the local population that, every now and then, they attempt to maintain the cooking at a certain standard, despite the streams of pilgrims.

In the previous century the grotto of the apparitions and the spring lay clearly beyond the city and, even today, they still nestle—in a park-like transition—against untamed nature. Three churches have arisen here which, piled on top of one another, cover with architecture the entire mountain from which the

Subversive Catholicism

grotto emerges. It is worth examining these churches closely. The common complaint as to the ugliness of Lourdes—a complaint which has already achieved the status of a truism, at least in bourgeois Catholic circles (which, as we know, are always closely tied to the last fashion but two)—also seems to apply to these churches. For that reason they have been abandoned to neglect and decay: for worship, the masses are steered into brutal, concrete hangars. Yet that does not change the fact that, for the majority of pilgrims to Lourdes, it is the enormous, piled-up basilica—the Mont Saint-Michel of the nineteenth century—that will be treasured as the essential image of their pilgrimage.

Above, on the mountain, stands the more slender edifice—with needle-point tower—of the Basilica of the Immaculate Conception, which is nonetheless the work of the important architect and conservator Viollet-le-Duc; it looks as though it was designed by the famous naïve painter Louis Vivin, who was also a railroad employee. Vivin's church elevations are notable for their decorative "stone-for-stone style." In order to view the interior it is perhaps best to take a child with you if you wish to obtain maximum enjoyment. Like a Christmas tree the grey walls are festooned with votive offerings. Golden hearts spell a phrase with the words of the apparition; weapons, epaulettes, and medals for bravery give witness to the gratitude of returned soldiers; burning hearts of silver look like grenades about to explode; standards and banners from all over the world decorate every free nook and cranny. The windows tell, in anecdotal classicism, the tale of Bernadette, such that the entire church is a house of gratitude and recollection for received graces: it feels almost like reading a large novel.

This church was placed over the first chapel of Lourdes, the crypt of today, which received the first pilgrims to Lourdes. In front of the crypt, however, there rises a gigantic crown that lies upon the dome of the underlying Basilica of the Rosary. Mighty bridges—reminiscent of the alignment of the Semmering railway—connect the various levels to each other; the fantasy of a model builder who wished to drive his trains between cathedrals appears to have been the guiding eye behind the entire complex. The substructures of these ramps embrace a large square in the middle of which appears, like an oriental dream, the façade of the Basilica of the Rosary, loosely based upon the façade of Saint Mark's in Venice. This church, a work of the architect Hardy, surely belongs among the most daring inventions of the late nineteenth century. A mighty Romanesque central construction made of light sandstone with three wide apses which each open into five chapels; the bright, colorful mosaics of these chapels—upon which shine invisible downlighters—glow from within the smooth stone that surrounds them. The enormous Virgin in the apse of the altar is a young Slavic girl from the "Ballet russes" clothed in an ermine of the fashion house Poiret, and even if the niche mosaics are not of the same quality as this astonishing work, their decorative function is too important for them to be allowed to fall from the wall in clumps. Hosts of pilgrims foregather in front of this mountain of a church for blessings and for the procession. Here, the language of shapes produced by the Eiffel Tower is once more successfully placed at the service of piety and religion.

The Ritual

Those who travel to Lourdes as faithful pilgrims do so less in order to pray there, and more in order to undertake certain specific actions and to allow the same to be done to them. This must not be misunderstood: there are certainly few places in the Catholic world where so many people undertake the apparently successful attempt to pray, together or alone. Yet prayer is essentially an internal act, even if it occurs loudly, and in Lourdes it appears to depend primarily upon combining these inner acts with external, almost objective procedures.

The Catholic religion has concentrated sacrifice entirely on the Mass and associated it, above all, with the crucifixion of

Jesus. The sacrificial customs of the pagans and the Jews are thereby, on the one hand, reinforced and also, on the other, replaced. The need to render gifts unto God and the saints—which in the face of the gulf between the receiver and the giver must forever remain only symbolic gifts—has however remained. The favored symbolic gifts are, generally, candles, yet it is probably in Lourdes that the apogee of candle-offering is to be experienced. If one were to take the time to add up all the many tons of wax that are melted in any one year in Lourdes, one would arrive at numbers that would pale in comparison with the sensual impression given by a world made from candles. Long streets are comprised of nothing but candle shops that sell candles in every shape and size, from pencil-thin to elephant's foot. Pyramids of candles burn before the grotto day and night. Those who offer them have only a short opportunity to see their own candle alight; it is barely lit before the guardian blows it out and puts it back in an enormous iron holder. Entire warehouses full of votive candles give confidence that, even in winter when there are fewer pilgrims, the sea of flames will never be extinguished.

Having offered your candle, you head to the bathhouse and join the long queue of the sick and healthy. You undress in cubicles made of blue-and-white striped canvas; behind a further curtain two strong helpers are waiting for you; they wear long blue aprons, and they plunge you into a bath which is filled with water from the holy spring. After being plunged, you make the sign of the cross, say a prayer and get dressed again, wet as you are.

At night, all pilgrims assemble for a procession with candles as was commanded by the apparition seen by Bernadette. The masses of people pass by one another with their candles held aloft, streams of pilgrims overtaking one another or moving in the opposite direction. This lends the motion something circular, infinite. The white statue of Mary looms above the candles; her long veil practically envelops her entire figure: only the round, childlike shoulders are discernible. Seen from behind,

A Magical Place: Lourdes and the Pilgrims

the swaying figure seems alive; it appears to be leading the procession. Countless sprays of carnations—wrapped in a great deal of cellophane—decorate the cage that protects her. Was it these flowers, tightly pressed against one another, that first reminded me of Benares? The long steps, the Ghats, which in Benares lead down to the sacred river, the Ganges. In the soft light of the morning the sound of bells and the smell of incense hang in the air; one hears the isolated singing of the monks and Sadhus. Beggars, the sick and the old with their crutches are everywhere. Near the bank fresh flowers and candles float along in tiny boats. The pilgrims await the rising of the sun in order to step into the water, to immerse themselves in it and thereby cleanse themselves of their sin.

Dare we call Lourdes a sort of "Catholic India"? Those who only focus on external appearances may find it absurd to compare the sober, neat town in the Pyrenees on its low, green, mountain river with the boiling chaos of Benares. The Catholic Church, which exercises the office of supervisor over Lourdes, provides an astounding organization for the floods of people and administers the miracle in strict orthodoxy, ever ready to suppress any atavistic religiosity. It is certainly not the doctrine, but the praxis which creates a connection between the two cities; it is the intriguingly natural sense of being at home in the forms of religion which allows a comparison of the pilgrims of the two cities. An English priest reports that it was on the Ghats of Benares that he made the decision to become a Catholic. At that moment he must also have thought of Lourdes.

Bernadette

At the beginning of the pilgrimage to Lourdes there stands the baffling figure of a young girl who possessed neither particular talent nor knowledge, who was sick and poorly nourished and accustomed to hard work from early childhood. Bernadette Soubirous was a member of that fourth estate which first arose after the revolution of 1848. She was also destined to lead a revolt against the bourgeois, liberal society, no less radical than the commune—even if using other means and totally without personal ambition. Her short life in the spotlight is documented down to the smallest detail, for her emergence entailed no small dilemma for the heads of the Church and State. The news of miracles was met with investigative commissions, "independent medical bodies" and observation committees. Doctors and police subjected Bernadette—as well as anyone who claimed to have experienced grace through the spring at Lourdes—to harrying inquisitions. The monomaniacal search for scientific proof, meanwhile, essentially only revealed how little the two opponents—the Church and the world—knew of each other. A Nobel prize winner's assessment of the miracles of Lourdes is just as unlikely to convince an unbeliever to believe in God as a scholastic proof of the same; for the intelligent sceptic has long since rejected science's claim to truth.

Bernadette was fourteen years old when, on the 11th of February 1858, she was sent by her mother to collect wood in the forest of Massabielle. Near a large grotto she was removing her shoes in order to wade through the millstream, when she saw a woman in the rock. "The woman wore a white dress, a white veil, a blue belt and a yellow rose on each foot," wrote Bernadette in her autobiography. The lady began to pray the rosary without moving her lips; Bernadette followed her example. Then she suddenly disappeared. Between February 11 and July 16, 1858, the white-clothed lady appeared eighteen times to Bernadette in the grotto. Ever larger numbers of people—thousands by the end—were witness to the ecstasies which overcame the shepherdess in the grotto. The initially silent apparition began to speak. "I do not promise to make you happy in this world, but in the next," was her first sentence. "Pray to God for sinners!" she ordered on another occasion. On February 25th she required Bernadette to wash her face in a spring, even though there was no spring there. The girl dug with her hands

A Magical Place: Lourdes and the Pilgrims

in the earth and suddenly water began to flow; that was the origin of the famous spring which since then has dispensed 120,000 liters of water daily.

The apparition told Bernadette to go to the priest and say to him that the people ought to come to her in procession and, at the end of her statement, she divulged her name. In the dialect of the Pyrenees she said: "Que soy era immaculada councepciou—I am the immaculate conception."—"That is incorrect," said the priest, as Bernadette repeated these words to him; she must have said, "I am the immaculately conceived," the priest asserted.

As the healings began, as the processions which the white lady had requested were held and the first chapel arose with the support of the Empress Eugenie, Bernadette disappeared into a cloister where she was treated with suspicion and subjected to pettiness. Before her death on April 16, 1879 she said: "You see, my story is quite simple. The Virgin used me. Then they put me in a corner. That is now my place, I am happy here and here I will remain."

One does not have to have seen the wax figure in the Musée Grevin of Lourdes—which shows Bernadette kneeling amidst sheep—to think of another shepherdess in French history who also heard heavenly voices in the forest. Joan of Arc came from Lorraine and Bernadette also hailed from a border region which was only lately appended to France. Both girls defended their message in the face of crushing intellectual and social superiority, both were subjected to interrogations and inquiries and remained simple and steadfast throughout. While Joan had fought against the external enemies of France, Bernadette's message applied to the internal enemies of the Church: she spoke of miracles and grace against a rationalistic theology, and urged processions and public prayer against the secularist state. In this bond between the mystical/grace-filled and the social/political, she is a very French saint.

Subversive Catholicism

The Pilgrims

Pilgrims pour through the streets of Lourdes in their thousands, all in the same direction: the grotto. It takes a while before one becomes aware of individuals within the mass. Older men and women sometimes bear a golden medallion, almost like a military decoration, on a light-blue silk ribbon. They are the long-time helpers who keep order around the bathhouses and the stands of candles. Ever more groups of helpers can be seen: Italian women with white nurse's caps and veils, like military orderlies from the First World War; the ladies of the Order of Malta in grey capes with a large Maltese cross; blue uniformed men, who wear harnesses around their shoulders to which the sick can cling; some wearing badges, some wearing armbands, and some wearing caps. Everywhere there are wheelchairs and, above all, the mode of transport unique to Lourdes: rickshaws with blue screens in which the sick can sit, protected from the weather, and which are pulled over the wide terrain by their helpers.

There are people lying in wheeled beds, simply staring at the grey sky with rigid eyes; people with excessively large legs and people with stick-thin legs; hunchbacks who can barely lift their heads, and invalids with powerful arms, who perhaps lost their legs in an accident. Nor have I forgotten the old parents accompanying a son with Down's Syndrome—brown-skinned Spanish farming folk in dark clothes—the son anemic and listening attentively to the explanations of his parents, energetically pointing out things to be seen; the African lady with many braids and almost blue-black skin who had bought a particularly white and particularly large Lady of Lourdes which she now held pressed against her body; the bent old priest in the blotchy soutane with a nut brown periwig; the corpulent young dwarf with oversized head who pushed a seriously ill child in a wheelchair through the melee; the two fat men carrying a candle which was as thick and long as a young tree; the elegant black woman from the Caribbean who held a large photo

A Magical Place: Lourdes and the Pilgrims

before her on which a man with scarred cheeks was to be seen—as the priest blessed the crowds she held the image up for the blessing.

Every afternoon the sick can receive the blessing in the large square in front of the two cathedrals which are piled on top of one another. Then a consecrated host is borne under a baldachino in a large procession to the sick who sit and lie in rows. The crowd moves forward with small steps; prayers drone from the loudspeakers in six different languages; only very occasionally one's nose picks up a hint of incense, but during the solemn blessing there suddenly reigns a profound silence, even though the sea of people seems almost beyond measure. The subterranean cathedral is as large as a velodrome, an oppressively engineered hall of naked concrete; it is here that the Masses for the sick are celebrated. The place is redolent of heroic pathos, severe bombast, and an imperialist aesthetic. Here, effect is achieved not with candles but with spotlights. The celebrants, in their vestments designed for maximum impact, have to cover large distances unaccompanied. The choir thunders out newly composed, Orff-like melodies that are meant to suggest something archaic. On his throne of concrete there sits a small Indian Cardinal, surrounded by twenty concelebrating priests. It is time for the Gospel to be read: the Deacon receives the blessing of the Cardinal and heads with the lectionary—which he holds above his head—toward the steps of the huge altar. Then, suddenly, a young man stands up out of his wheelchair. He looms over the other invalids and is visible to all. His fists clenched, he begins a concentrated boxing match with the air. He now thrashes an unseen opponent, as if possessed. Then he relaxes back into a more moderate tempo, as if he were simply training. He is completely absorbed in his fight. Surrounded by ten thousand, he is yet completely alone. There, enthroned high above, sits the Cardinal; far away from the young boxer in the blue windcheater, but just as clearly elevated above the rest. The Deacon reads a passage from Jesus's farewell words. The

Subversive Catholicism

blue boxer boxes. Every one of his punches is a perfect hit. "I will no longer talk much with you, for the prince of this world is coming," reads the Deacon. "He has no power over me, but I do as the Father has commanded me, so that the world may know that I love the Father." For an instant it seems as if the Deacon had proclaimed the Gospel just for the two men; for the red man who sits, unmoving, and for the blue man, absorbed in his fight amidst the crowd.

The House of Bernadette's Parents

The small house in which Bernadette Soubirous lived constitutes the last remaining thing that recalls the old Lourdes. Like the small house that Nietzsche rented in Sils Maria, it stands sandwiched between two palatial hotels. Bernadette was born in the Boly Mill; later, as the family sank into misfortune, they had to leave the mill and went into the *"cachot,"* a small erstwhile prison. There Bernadette lived until the time of the apparitions. Thereafter the Bishop of Tarbes arranged for the Soubirous family to move into a somewhat more livable house, once again a mill, in which Bernadette remained until her entry into the cloister. This "maison paternelle," as is painted in enormous letters on the external wall, today contains the majority of the traces of the Soubirous family, even though a plenitude of votive offerings has made the narrow rooms into a sanctuary. Yet the crutches a grateful visitor has hung on the wall, the candles that stand burning in the fireplace, the many small marble tablets with the word "merci" carved onto them do not disturb the private atmosphere: they blend into the whole, as though the occupiers themselves had left these things there. The Soubirous were very poor people. Their abode perhaps indicates this better than any description of the economic catastrophes that befell Miller Soubirous. The rooms are low and narrow. The parents shared two small rooms with nine children, five of whom lived into adulthood. Thick stone walls turned these houses into caves,

A Magical Place: Lourdes and the Pilgrims

into which very little light penetrated. We know that these houses were damp and could barely be warmed by the wood that was collected.

There is no way of glorifying that life: a glimpse of the black, stone gutter in the kitchen would convince even the most fatuous romantic of the hardship associated with life in the mill. And yet we are struck with envy here in the rooms of Bernadette's parental home. The great Italian essayist Mario Praz, in his *Filosofia del arredamento*, described the houses of old Europe: the human proportions, their materials forged by tradition, their eloquent order. Praz naturally occupied himself with the palaces and apartments of those citizens who are documented by oil paintings and watercolors, yet he would certainly have been enchanted by the house of Bernadette's parents. On a cracked, uneven terrazzo floor there stand small chairs, their braided straw seats long since stripped by relic hunters. Against the walls stand the beds, with a countrified Empire-style frame. Over each bed there is a small wooden canopy, from which hang curtains of red and white gingham. Bernadette's bed is behind glass because it is so cut and gnawed that, on first glance, one might think one was looking at some sort of audacious carving; the relic hunters have been here too.

What are most beautiful are the walls. They have the sort of grey which one of the most significant painters of the seventeenth century, Louis Le Nain, discovered on the walls of peasants' abject hovels; Le Nain's depiction of the latter anticipates the house of Bernadette's parents. No decorator would be able to reproduce the shimmering grey of these crooked walls. However, the devotional visitors have left their mark here too, this time by way of addition: every centimeter is covered in pencil, which spreads a silvery spider's web over the plaster. An old photo shows a sister-in-law of Bernadette's sitting on one of the canopy beds reading the newspaper *Les Pyrénées*. The room then looked exactly as it does today; apart from the protective glass walls, no later hand has introduced any sug-

Subversive Catholicism

gestion of a museum. In a magnificent plaster frame, its corners the worse for wear, there is a photo of the young Bernadette: she wears a black and white striped headscarf strangely reminiscent of Arabia and stares out almost gloomily from her southern child's face, as if she had now understood what the white lady meant when she prophesied no happiness for her here on earth. It was here in this room that she bade farewell to her parents, and here that her father died without having once visited his daughter in the cloister. An extraordinary fate has protected this most ordinary of abodes from vanishing. It can still be sensed here: the life of poor, god-fearing peasants that once formed the backdrop for the overpowering wealth of images of European culture.

Kitsch

One of the first Lourdes grottoes was cobbled together by Bernadette herself. There was even the plaster figure of the Immaculata and a kneeling Bernadette, which only needed to be placed in a grotto of bark and small pieces of charcoal. At that time Lourdes grottoes could be found everywhere across the Catholic world—within cloistered gardens, in country cemeteries, in private chapels, nestled against the external walls of a church or in the vestibule of religious houses. Whether in Cusco or Lodz, Londonderry or Madras it was always the grotto that gave witness to the re-vivified Roman Church under Saint Pius X. Among the artificial rocks, often reminiscent of the open-air enclosures of zoological gardens—the same cliffs of cement, stucco, or pumice that surrounded the fabulous "Catholic" Queen Louise of Prussia—the Madonna of Lourdes was displayed in her blue and white bridesmaid's robe. Even within the gardens of the Vatican the Lourdes grotto was instituted to replace the arboreal frivolities of previous centuries.

Why did the Virgin not appear in the Middle Ages? The artists of that time would have been a match for her appearance. Instead she showed herself to the eyes of a human being in a

A Magical Place: Lourdes and the Pilgrims

poor, remote region in the middle of the industrial age. No one managed to come up with an adequate depiction; instead, the production-line took over. I first saw the plastic bottle in the form of the Virgin with the small blue crown as a twist-cap in a fridge in Naples; when the fridge rattled into life the small water-filled statuette softly shook along with it. In Lourdes it became clear to me that that plastic figurine had millions of sisters—Madonnas of all sizes, always with the removable crown. In every devotional supermarket there stood boxes full of them, all ready for the invasion of pilgrims. A quiet "Alleluia" or "Gloria in excelsis" rained down from hidden loud speakers on the hapless clients, eagerly rummaging through the heap of Madonnas, and yet hamstrung by the oft-observed indecision in the face of such a superfluity.

Joris-Karl Huysmans—who, full of rage, saw in Lourdes the opportunity for a new, gothic religiosity disappearing under the mountains of malicious, industrial ugliness—claimed that the traders in devotional goods in Lourdes were almost exclusively Jews. Even if he had been correct, he would have had to admit that they had apparently hit upon the Catholic taste. There is always a ready market for little wooden shoes incorporating an image of the Madonna. The Grotto in a flurry of snow is exquisitely completed by Bernadette as a nun, made from marzipan so that her head can be bitten off. The green and yellow bottles filled with the liqueur of the house of Izarra sparkle like church windows next to a forest of crucifixes. Pyrenean honey is sweet and healthy and not quite as tacky as the utterly plastic color photograph of a blood-smeared Christ, who opens and shuts his blue eyes in the constant fight for his life.

Is kitsch only a Catholic sickness? In India, large placards advertise baby food with the new-born Shiva, while Tibetan dragons hover threateningly in aniline colors; new Russian and Greek icons shine like glassy transfer prints; new mosques resemble hotels in California.

Our century apparently has an unharmonious relationship

to every religion. When our age comes into contact with the faith of more pious, simpler people, there arises a reaction which is comparable to the struggles and resistance with which the body fights blood of the wrong blood group. This reaction is religious kitsch—it characterizes the clash of a secularized civilization with the sense of veneration and faith of those people who, at the same time, originate from within this very civilization. Thus the kitsch in a place like Lourdes is probably unavoidable. It is the last final memory of a time when the greatest artists vied with one another to unleash a truly inebriating sense of beauty within churches, before the very eyes of the poor. The sour, self-consciously "objective," puritanical ideal of "noble simplicity," encouraged in official church art, will never be able to silence this memory. Kitsch is inauthentic, certainly, but it stands for something authentic. It is the defiant resistance of the poor in an age which despises their needs.

The Grotto

The grotto of Lourdes is a beautiful rock formation, almost poured from a mold, a monolithic rock-fault which does not lead particularly deep into the mountain. In its hind-most crevasse lies the source of the spring: one looks through a glass plate upon an illuminated stream of water, surrounded by green leaves, a somewhat aquarium-like view. Half way up stands a statue of the Immaculata, made from Carrara marble, as the travel guides for Lourdes never fail to mention. The square before the grotto is a paved slope that covers the entire area between the mountain and the fast-flowing river. Here all day stands a dense crowd waiting to be led through barriers into the grotto. The people grope their way through the grotto with both hands, in a long line; many do not let go of the wall for the entire length of the path. Where a small amount of moisture runs over the walls, they press their faces to the rock in order to refresh themselves with a few drops. Prayers are spo-

A Magical Place: Lourdes and the Pilgrims

ken through the loudspeaker; occasionally there is the voice of a muffled Chaliapin or a stifled Gigli. The people only speak in muted tones. Even the uninitiated would notice that, on the field between the grotto and the green-colored Gave which shoots past it, a palpable tension prevails.

In the eyes of religious scholars, the grotto of Lourdes is only the latest example in a long line of mystical caverns. In all religions the cave is the place of entrance into the other world, into heaven or into hell. Priestesses guarded the doors to the underworld in Delphi and Cumae; there man encountered the gods and the dead, experienced healing and advice, and brought sacrifices. Christ was born in a cave in Bethlehem, and St John received his vision of the mysterious revelation in a cave in Patmos. The holy spring, the nymphaeum, also has a long history among the religions of the world. What is remarkable, therefore, is that the grotto of Lourdes was not a site of veneration since prehistoric times that was then—as is sometimes the case—given a new significance by Christianity. Bernadette was no religious scholar. She did not seek out the grotto for it religious suitability. She was a fourteen-year-old, uneducated girl and could not have imagined—even for a moment—that her experience would ever be compared with something else that had occurred before. It can even be said with complete certainty that the concept of the immaculate conception that the apparition used was completely unknown to her: it was not even long in use, as Pope Pius IX had only first pronounced the dogma of the Virgin conceived without original sin in 1854. Bernadette was ten years old at the time.

Correctly understood, this dogma has less to do with Mary than with Christ: it is a definition of the belief in the divinity of Jesus and relates to the idea that a human being impaired by original sin could not have been the Mother of God. Thus Lourdes, with its spring which washes away sins and sickness, is actually less a site of Marian pilgrimage and more a pilgrimage to Christ. That the Church wishes to suggest this interpretation is shown by the entire site, with its interplay of architecture and natural features. In the visions of Ezekiel there is a verse which is sung during the sprinkling of the new holy water at Easter, the "Vidi aquam": "I saw water flowing from the right side of the temple, and all to whom this water flowed were healed and sang, alleluia." The Christian interpretation saw in this Old Testament text a description of the dead Christ on the cross, from whose wound on the right hand side water flowed: the baptismal water for the forgiveness of sins. It is as if this verse forms the basis for the architectural plan for the sanctuary of Lourdes. Seen from the front of the church mount, the "temple," the grotto with its spring lies on the right-hand side, underneath the nave of the upper basilica, the foundations of which comprise the cliffs which lie above the grotto. Thus in the language of religious symbols, the mountain—with its connected churches—portrays the body of Christ, and the grotto the wound in His side. From this wound runs the water. Those who have attained insight into their own imperfection bathe in this water. Could not this insight be seen as the first sign, at least, of spiritual health?

In Praise of the Lourdes Madonna

I saw my first Lourdes Madonna as a small boy in the house of winegrowers in the Rheingau; my parents were sampling wine downstairs in the kitchen while the daughter of the house, who was as old as I was, showed me the rooms of the upper levels. The bedroom of her parents lay there in solemn, chilly solidity; the eiderdown was enormously plumped up and so hard it could have been filled with cement; the pillows had sharp creases in the middle which gave them two stiff rabbit's ears; and there She stood, on an old chest of drawers opposite the bed, like an ice princess amidst all this frigidity, yet strangely alive with her small, tenderly made-up puppet face. My mother smiled ironically as I told her of the figure which appeared so beautiful to me: she was, she said, a "table-top saint."

Yet soon thereafter I saw my next Lourdes Madonna in another locale, somewhat larger than the one in the rural bedroom: a very small one, barely larger than a chess piece, yet always with the same inclination of the head and the flowing folds of the white garment that was neither a dress nor an antique tunic, nothing removable, but something all of a piece with the body. I learnt that the individual Lourdes Madonnas that I encountered were the emissaries of a large population of Madonnas that had settled all over the earth. Their bodies had peculiar proportions; the legs had to be over-long as though drawn by William Blake or Füssli, the torso was flat—no feminine bulge to be seen. The face was childlike, with a clear, high forehead of balanced, Raffaelesque proportions—perhaps a little too balanced because, as we know, the most beautiful faces are never completely symmetrical. The blue belt fluttered lightly and the folds of the garment were likewise pressed against the body—as though by a gust of wind—which gave the form a sense of movement, as though she were floating toward the viewer. One could even see feet in small slippers underneath the hem, but the figure was actually more like the statuettes of those ladies of the Japanese court who hid their feet and seem to move along on the seams of their kimonos. Although all the statues I encountered were painted with thick oil paint, like a horse on a fairground carousel, there was no doubt what they were made of: plaster; and often they were a little battered as the white plaster often peeped out, crumbly and dry.

In the old churches of France—desecrated during the revolution and, in the nineteenth century, more often poorly restored than correctly refitted—one could always see plaster representations of this little tribe ranged along the wall; they were meant to replace the destroyed gothic sculptures: there were St Louis, the Curé of Ars, the Virgin of Orléans, and, naturally, the Lourdes Madonna. There she had a society into which she fitted rather well, but in the baroque German churches with their well-preserved, ostentatious decoration—or in modern concrete churches—she was like a foreign body, usually bashfully placed in a side chapel near the entrance. The faithful, by the way, did not appear to notice this awkwardness: there were often too many candles burning in front of her. Plaster was not the only material from which she was made: the Lourdes Madonna was also extant in plastic and even in glass, as a bottle for Lourdes water with her crown as a stopper. At her feet, in convent corridors, one could find a half-dried African violet and a grateful cactus, yet her true home was an artificial grotto, a successor to the baroque mussel-grottoes of princely palaces; for, to Bernadette, the little shepherdess, our Blessed Lady of Lourdes appeared, like an antique water nymph, in a grotto, which was then replicated in many places in pumice—like the landscaping for a miniature electric train.

Lourdes grottoes abounded, not just in the Vatican alongside

In Praise of the Lourdes Madonna

Renaissance palazzetti, but also in the heart of dangerous, violent metropolises: in Cairo and New York, in Seoul and Bogotà, but also in the churchyards where the constant honking of the unceasing stream of traffic was somewhat muted; the grotto was also a natural collage for the walls of huge apartment blocks. And in front of these caves there were always a couple of people, even when the church itself was shut; red carnations in cellophane bags hung on the railings surrounding the grotto; here too candles burned and the people stared into the gloom of the cave where, high above, the white-lacquered statue stood, like a Catholic version of Queen Louise of Prussia. The large blue mantle from classic Marian images was reduced to the light-blue belt, like the blue band that secured the white diapers of very small girls before the American pink appeared. Why, I asked myself, did our Blessed Lady of Lourdes not appear a few hundred years earlier to the greatest of all religious painters, the Florentine Fra Angelico? What could Fra Angelico have done with a flowing white garment, bound with a ribbon of blue—can't you just imagine it? But she came later, indeed during our own age, for her mission was of a different kind. In any case she clearly did not intend to become a piece of art.

The ironic smile of my mother announced it to me at the time: in our milieu, among educated, art-loving people who read, the Lourdes Madonna was not to be taken seriously. It was kitsch.

Kitsch, to this very day, is a popular word, almost indispensable when it comes to aesthetic judgements. It is not a particularly old word, first appearing around 1860—was there no kitsch beforehand? Are we to imagine that there was nothing poorly imitated, tasteless, soullessly artificial, pseudo, and inauthentic in the eighteenth century? Perhaps there was, but it was not yet kitsch. Kitsch presupposes the final demise of the craftsman's secure sense of taste—a kind of inherited instinct, the capacity to draw upon long experience of working with the material of his craft and elicit the laws of proportion that lie hidden within it. Industrial production, no longer bound to the laws of the craftsman's material, now prevailed.

Yet man is slower than technical development, with his dreams and his standards, and he has remained, even to this day, captive to the lost pre-industrial millennia, back in the grey dawn before the present time. He contemplates seductive ideas: is our separation from the inherited concept of beauty, from proportions which have grown organically from the material, really so final? Could one not shrewdly combine the positive aspects of both the old and new age? Isn't it possible, using machines that, per se, do not have to be hostile to beauty, to create art that is beautiful in the old sense? With far less effort and much greater perfection? And for the benefit of far more people than previously, when art was only available in disreputable exclusivity for the few? Thus began the whole business of mass-production, the stamping, pouring, and punching of Lourdes Madonnas—and of so much else.

It is truly an experience when one first comes across such a herd of Madonnas in one of the thousands of devotional stalls in Lourdes; a cloned populace of absorbed prayers, ranging from two meters to two centimeters in size. As well as experiencing a slight crawling of the flesh at this sight, I also realized that this plenitude of Madonnas representing the Marian apparition is *not a bad thing*; on the contrary. Do we not already encounter, in the Catholic world, the duplicated Madonna? The various black Madonnas and the one of Guadalupe, of La Salette, of Altötting, of Kevelaer and of the Pillar, of Pompeii and of Loretto—each one different, and yet ever the same? Of course it is not always like this: I had the opportunity, during a visit to a large sculpture studio, to see Michelangelo's David in its original size—in spotless Carrara marble—*twelve of them*, standing one behind the other. They had been ordered for an American chain of hotels and, for me, that was the end of David; he has still not recovered from this cruel treatment. You see, kitsch is a complicated thing. It is a symptom of many things, even of society's fears.

In Praise of the Lourdes Madonna

The bourgeois social climber—and which of us, at some time or another, has not been that?—fears kitsch, because he could find himself exposed in his lack of taste. Our pauperist and minimalist interiors express the fear that, given greater opulence, we might fall into the kitsch-trap and see ourselves brought before the judges of petit bourgeois taste. Naturally there is no danger of this in an empty room. But kitsch is strong and in our world survives even the most rigid preventative measures. We have long been familiar with naked kitsch, sour kitsch, green kitsch, shocking kitsch and authenticity-kitsch; and each of these variations is far more difficult to detect and, for its identification, requires a considerably more honed sensibility than that required by the Lourdes Madonna in her unprotected, naïve innocence. She does not protect herself, the Lourdes Madonna, but she can protect others: Cordelia Spaemann, the deceased wife of the philosopher Robert Spaemann, said that the devotional kitsch of places of pilgrimage, at the summit of which stands the Lourdes Madonna, is the protective wall that keeps the smug aesthetes—she called them the "pack of aesthetes"—away from the sanctuary.

Let us—with appropriate uncouthness—push to one side the whole question of kitsch and the Lourdes Madonna and fix upon the naked fact that, in the whole of the twentieth century, there was not one single artistic or handicraft creation that was as distinctive, universally comprehensible, nation- and culture-transcending, functional in a liturgical sense and identifiably Catholic as the Lourdes Madonna. Her anonymous creator possessed the same form-creating genius as the inventor of Mickey Mouse and the designer of the Coca-Cola label. Where the Lourdes Madonna is, there is the Catholic Church. In the face of such assertive power—and how gentle a power!—every taste verdict about her shrivels to the inconsequential level of personal opinion on beauty or ugliness.

Since the beginning of her second millennium the Latin Church at first gradually, then with increasing pace and emphasis, sundered herself from the traditional images of the

Subversive Catholicism

ancient Church. It is worth recapitulating, in a few words, the steps along this path. We have become accustomed to view this path as a grand liberation from the prison of prescription and restriction; the development of religious art is celebrated almost as a tale of progress. In the beginning there stood the icon, and strict laws governed it. It placed the appearance of the saints—at the summit of which were the Panagia and the Redeemer—within rigid, immovable rules and removed them from the realm of subjective interpretation. It largely disclaimed the perspectivity and plasticity of depiction which had long since been achieved in Hellenistic painting; it pursued two-dimensionality. Its chromaticity was equally fixed: which colors were for Christ and which for Mary, which colors were accorded to the world of the Old Covenant and which to the New, which drapery corresponded to which depiction of which situation, which accompanying figures, which props and which emblems were allowed to appear—or rather, which *had to* appear—these were as little up to the painter's personal decision as the prayers he was bound to pray as he crushed up his colors or applied layers of paint to the wooden tablet. These icons were not the pious decorations of a church, but rather certain signs of divine presence, of the same rank as the presence of the consecrated host in the tabernacle. Their two-dimensionality was not due to the artist's lack of skill: rather, it showed that the figure portrayed no longer belonged to the realm of the sensually tangible, but instead peered through the window that is the icon's frame, from eternity into temporality.

Let us set aside the particular reasons why the Latin Church abandoned its shared visual tradition with the Greek Church; let us accept that she did so and headed down the path of a great adventure which led painting to ever new triumphs; whether it was also to the advantage of the liturgical image is a question for another day. Everyone knows the stages of this particular liberation: Giotto's conquest of a new form of corporeality introduced a process through which all phases of the contemporary adaptation of biblical material and biblical

In Praise of the Lourdes Madonna

forms have passed through the centuries. The artists occasionally became willful theologians, basing their images on their own personal interpretation of the events in the history of salvation. They were story tellers who did not shy away from the anecdotal. They took the biblical material as the mere pretext for ever-more brilliant paintings. They became theatrical producers or even opera directors, who staged the stations of Jesus's life according to current taste. They sublimated or banalized the lives of saints, situating them on platforms of clouds or in grim cells. And after everything had been tried and what was regarded as the "emancipation from ecclesial patronage" was firmly under way, the official rupture came: Western art bade farewell to its most generous and patient of patrons and turned to other tasks. Behind there remained a Church that was intimidated and confused, which saw itself forcibly ejected from the principal aesthetic current of the age and found itself having to make do with the remaining vestiges of the artisan industry and pale imitations of the transient fashions of the day.

This is the end of the unique path of Western religious art. The deregulation of ecclesial art and its surrender to individualism and subjectivism has finally led to a fundamental sundering of art from the Church. Even after more than a century of such a development this has not yet become clear to the most elevated levels of the hierarchy—papal advisors on art and similarly venerable institutions—yet it has been clear to the faithful people for at least that length of time. Without the help of any slogans or mottos, a turn to the veneration of images has taken place among the faithful: it could be characterized as a "re-iconization." The multinational population of Catholics turned itself to face sacred images which are not works of art and which do not intend to be. Goethe did not know how right he was when, in his *Roman Elegies*, he wrote in a spiteful undertone: "Miraculous images are usually very poor paintings." Idols are not meant to be works of art, and even when they are—like the great icons of Byzantium and

Subversive Catholicism

Russia—they are only incidentally so. The Orthodox would presumably forbid anyone to call the Lourdes Madonna an icon; the fact that she is a statue would already be held against her, for the Orthodox apply the Old Testament proscription of images to "simulacra" or three-dimensional divine images.

Yet, in a non-technical sense, the Lourdes Madonna may be called an icon; the icon of the West, created by an anonymous hand, establishing a type, a perennial manifestation. As an item of mass-production she is radically un-individualistic, almost anti-subjectivist. She is just as far removed from the great art of old Europe as she is from the art of the twentieth century. For advanced art critics of the nineteenth century she was "parlormaid's art"; for the liturgy experts of the twentieth century she is fit only for Poles and Africans. This augurs well for her viability.

Due to her effect, we dubbed the Lourdes Madonna an icon; this effect cannot be compared with any piece of art made for a church during the twentieth century. Yet the Lourdes Madonna has a claim to the honorary title of icon for yet more profound and weighty reasons; from the point of view of her genesis she matches the highest demands that can be made of an icon. The ideal of immutability, of suppressing the contemporary, the personal, and the personally inspired—which we associate with the icon—does not arise from an oriental, anti-individual disposition, a quasi-Egyptian torpor, but rather is intimately connected with the emergence of a Christian form of art and the particular conditions inherent in it. Before the genesis of all Christian painting and the veneration of images stands the imposing hurdle already alluded to: the proscription of images by the Old Covenant, expressed in the second commandment—not simply a cultic provision which is subject to its time, but rather a law spoken by God Himself. For the early Christians—who originated in no small proportion from among the Jewish people—this commandment was all the more evident since the religions of the pagans, with their superfluity of magnificent statues of gods, were religions of images. Christianity too was destined to be a religion of images, but for this it required authorization that could not be given by men—God Himself had to lift the ban on images, and he had indeed done so: Paul was the first to express it as he named Jesus Christ "the image of God." The incarnate God permitted human eyes to take possession of His form; that was after all but one aspect of His manifold self-surrender to man. Nonetheless, the reluctance to paint this man Jesus in the same way as the uniquely beautiful mummy portraits of Fayum, which appeared in nearby Egypt while he was upon the earth, would have been insuperable, had there not been an image of Jesus that did not originate from human hands and which remained as a witness to the Savior's earthly life. We are referring to that piece of linen which Goethe—in his *West-East Divan*—named the "cloth of all cloths" upon which "the image of the Lord impressed itself." This shadowy impression, this portrait-like depiction which had come into existence in an unartistic way, without brush and paint—this mysterious image stands at the origin of all Christian painting. This cloth of all cloths is the foundation for the face of Christ that was constantly preserved over hundreds of years until Michelangelo tore himself from it in an act of violence.

Here lies the basis for the strict conditions required for an icon: it is an image endowed by God; who would dare to change it? The notion that a liturgical image, an image for the service of God, ought always to be an image endowed by God Himself, something man has been given, not something made by him—this view remains alive in the Christian East. Here there are icons of particular dignity, which according to tradition were not painted by human hands—*acheiropoetos* they are called (Greek: "not made by hands"), and they shine among the many icons created by nameless artists—icons which themselves ought also to be dubbed *acheiropoetos*—and which were similarly painted according to the archetype of such images.

Is it not astounding the degree to which the Lourdes Madonna corresponds to such a conception of the Christian

Subversive Catholicism

image—this industrial product, which initially seems to stand in supposedly stark contrast to the venerable images of early Christianity? She does not exist thanks to artistic invention, but rather to the vision of a saint who had described how in a cave that "white lady," as she called her, confronted her and introduced herself in the dialect of the Pyrenees as "Immaculate Conception"—not, mind you, as "the One immaculately conceived," but rather as an abstract concept ("the Immaculate Conception," an abstract noun) in human form, as the incarnation of a *word*. Then, following the description given by the shepherd girl, some model-maker in a factory of devotional wares—or perhaps even several men, whose names in all likelihood no one could ever discover—created this statue as the "vera icon," the true image of the apparition which since then has run off the production line in its hundreds of thousands. Truly *acheiropoetos* with her non-individual lineaments, like a puppet—similar to all people and to none—as is appropriate to the first human being of the new creation, the perfectly new Eve. Who would dare to claim that we deserve better?

About the Author

MARTIN MOSEBACH, born in Frankfurt am Main, studied law, and has published eleven novels, many short stories, essays, poems, scripts for dramas, opera libretti, theater pieces, and radio plays. He is actively engaged in dialogue on contemporary issues through contributions to daily papers and magazines. Apart from many other awards, he was honored in 2007 with Germany's foremost literary award, the "Georg-Büchner-Preis," in 2013 with the "Literature-Award of the Konrad-Adenauer-Foundation," and in 2015 with the "Goethe-Award of the City of Frankfurt am Main." His most recent books include *The Heresy of Formlessness: The Roman Liturgy and Its Enemy* (Angelico, 2018), and *The 21: A Journey into the Land of Coptic Martyrs* (Plough, 2019).

Printed in Great Britain
by Amazon